W9-BMH-682

Realistic Decoys

Carving, Texturing, Painting & Finishing

Keith Bridenhagen & Patrick Spielman

 Sterling Publishing Co. Inc. New York

To Christine and Patricia—for their support and enduring patience

Edited and designed by Barbara Busch

Library of Congress Cataloging in Publication Data
Bridenhagen, Keith.
    Realistic decoys.

    Bibliography: p.
    Includes index.
        1. Decoys (Hunting) 2. Wood-carving—Technique.
3. Painting—Technique. I. Spielman, Patrick E.
II. Title.
NK9704.B75   1984   745.593   84-8608
ISBN 0-8069-7908-9 (pbk.)

5   7   9   10   8   6   4

Copyright © 1984 by Patrick Spielman
Published by Sterling Publishing Co., Inc.
Two Park Avenue, New York, N.Y. 10016
Distributed in Canada by Oak Tree Press Ltd.
% Canadian Manda Group, P.O. Box 920, Station U
Toronto, Ontario, Canada M8Z 5P9
Distributed in the United Kingdom by Blandford Press
Link House, West Street, Poole, Dorset BH15 1LL, England
Distributed in Australia by Capricorn Ltd.
P.O. Box 665, Lane Cove, NSW 2066
Manufactured in the United States of America
All rights reserved

Acknowledgments

The authors express their sincerest appreciation and gratitude to a number of individuals who in a variety of ways contributed to the eventuality of this book. We thank Eric Beckstrom for his interest and the use of his workshop. Thanks to Bob Spielman for handling some pressing business obligations during this writing. We are grateful to Kevin Kelly of Fish Creek, Wisconsin, and to Reeve's Taxidermy, Carlisle, Arkansas for their mounts. We extend special gratitude to the following who not only afforded us support and encouragement but also loaned us decoys from their personal collections for us to photograph: Tom "Shipwreck" Kelly, William and "Bridie" Hickman, and Dennis and Teresa Parravano. Many thanks with much appreciation to Harold Schopf for sharing his knowledge and sources, and for his encouragement. Some helpful photos were provided by Jim Legault, Colwood Electronics, Foredom Power Tools, Hot Tools, and the Oscar Johnston Wildlife Gallery. We also want to recognize the Milwaukee Public Museum for providing information. We appreciated the cooperation from Harmann Studios and our prompt, efficient typist, Julie Kaczmarek. Most important, we acknowledge the sacrifices endured by our families during this work. Their understanding and support was especially helpful.

CONTENTS

Color section between pages 64 and 65

Illus. 1. A black duck carved in a realistic texture and pose. Here the carving shows the duck about to preen. Photo by Jim Legault.

Introduction

It's doubtful if there is any other area of woodcarving currently as popular, as interesting, as challenging, or more satisfying than decoy carving. Carvings of this age-old art can be made as plain or basic as one wants, or they may be carved and painted so that they are extraordinarily detailed, lifelike creations (Illus. 1 and 2). For the most part, *Realistic Decoys* deals with the essential techniques employed to produce realistic decoy carvings. You will learn how to make carvings that are anatomically correct in shape and proportions with carved and textured feathers, and so on—all appropriately painted to match nature's own designs.

The primary purpose of this book is to clearly and methodically lead the carver through those techniques necessary to achieve some reasonable proficiency at the upper level of this art form. Every effort was made to provide as many clear closeup illustrations as possible so that details could be closely observed and understood (Illus. 3). However, it must be stated here at the onset that there is no better substitute for learning about duck details than actually observing and studying live ducks in their natural habitat. Early in the book you will learn that a duck's appearance is not always consistent. It changes and often docs so dramatically from season to season or moment to moment with the changes in behavior and environment.

Illus. 2. Two examples of "Realistic Decoys." At right is a goldeneye carved in natural butternut with minimum feather detailing. At left is a totally feather carved, textured and realistically painted version of the ever-popular mallard drake.

Illus. 3. This close-up shows one area of surface detailing on the mallard decoy shown in Illus. 2. Note the delicate carved feather texturing, the subtle and gradual changes in color and tone typical of this and many other ducks.

The successful carver knows all of the little peculiarities as well as the obvious behaviors and poses. Consequently, serious attention to detail is of major importance. The authors have made a straightforward attempt to help the carver become aware of those tangible details by accentuating little observed intricacies with word and photographic examples.

These special procedures and techniques are presented here in a logical sequential order. They will lead the carver through every step surely and confidently until his ultimate creation becomes a visual reality.

Essentially the material covered in this book does not duplicate the basic or beginning procedures and techniques found in the preceding book, *Making Wood Decoys* (Sterling Publishing Co., Inc., New York, 1982). If necessary, refer to this beginner's book for information about cutting out, shaping, smoothing, and other basic finishing details. And, due to limited space, this book does not contain patterns and plans. A new, separate, companion volume, *Decoy Pattern Book*, by Keith Bridenhagen (Sterling Publishing Co., Inc., forthcoming) contains all of the plans and specifications for over thirty ducks in both male and female genders for most common species.

Successful creative decoy carving requires more than just the ability to reproduce profile outlines and three-dimensional shapes. It's much more than just painting on blotches of colors that are common to a specific duck. The many and varied surfaces of a duck's body, and feather shapes, for example, must be systematically and realistically carved—feather by feather—and meticulously textured—vane by vane. Feathers must then be painted appropriately. The final work often displays gradual, subtle changes and delicate transitions in tone and texture as one's eye travels over the surface of the carving from bill to tail (Illus. 3).

Eight pages of full color are included to give the reader/carver some examples of texturing and examples of the kind of colorings involved in realistic decoy painting. These color photos, though immensely helpful, illustrate only a few different ducks and are intended only as typical examples. They actually show the end results, but space permits illustrating only the detailed carving of a canvasback, bluebill, and the popular mallard drake.

Fortunately, there are a number of good, complete references and other support publications available that illustrate and deal heavily with correct shapes and coloring of virtually any species. These books should be used if you are not able to view and study live ducks or mounted specimens. See Illus. 4. Some of these recommended references and helpful guides are listed in the Bibliography in the appendix. The appendix also lists sources for special supplies such as eyes, cast-lead feet, and study bills, as well as some sources for special carving blocks, and precarved kits.

Once you get into this fascinating art form of creating lifelike decoy carvings, in all probability, you will want to join clubs, enter contests, and know of associations dealing with decoy carving and the preservation of duck habitat. Appropriate periodicals are also listed for such sources of current and timely information.

Realistic Decoys is for that special breed of woodworking artist/ craftsperson. It is prepared for those who can learn to thrive on perfection while expressing the wonders of nature in the execution of carvings exhibiting realism and beauty.

Illus. 4. The creative decoy carver's workbench is more often cluttered with visual aids and references than with a vast selection of sophisticated tools. Here the carver refers to photographic sources for assistance in feather layout on the pintail (in progress) that is being carved from tupelo wood.

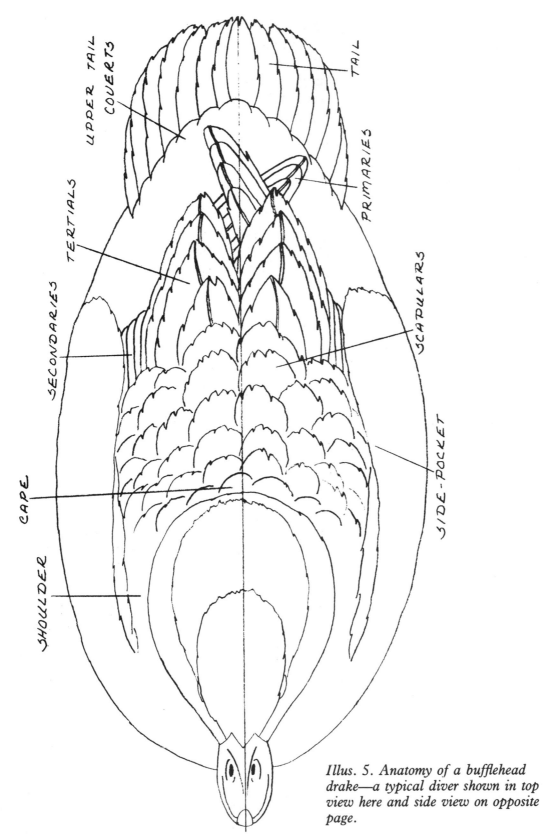

UPPER TAIL COVERTS

TAIL

TERTIALS

PRIMARIES

SECONDARIES

SCAPULARS

CAPE

SIDE-POCKET

SHOULDER

Illus. 5. Anatomy of a bufflehead drake—a typical diver shown in top view here and side view on opposite page.

10

1. Anatomy—Divers Versus Dabblers

The physical structure of ducks can pretty well be categorized according to their life-style. Essentially, most ducks fall into one of two distinct groups: divers or dabblers.

Divers (Illus. 5) are bottom feeders and they are found on larger bodies of water. Their food consists of animal matter such as clams, snails, crayfish, leeches, and so on.

Dabblers (Illus. 6), on the other hand, are primarily surface feeders. They are found on ponds, rivers, and small lakes. Their food consists of weeds, seeds, and grains that grow on or near the surface of the water. It is not unusual to see dabblers feeding in open grain fields far from any sight of water.

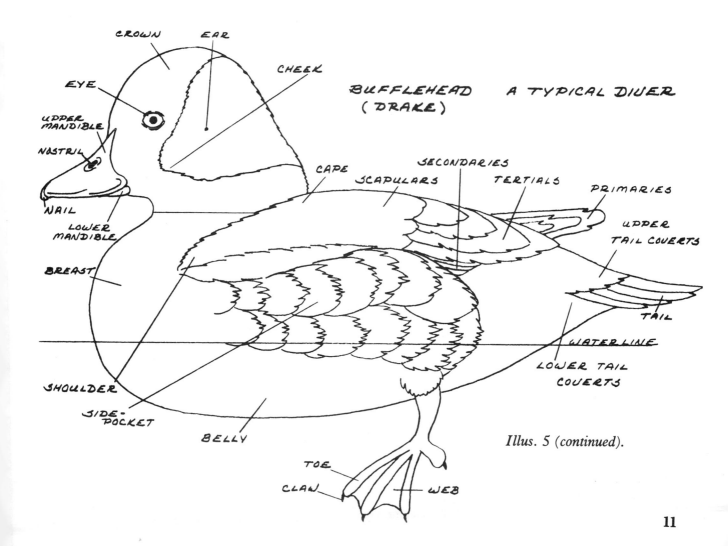

Illus. 5 (continued).

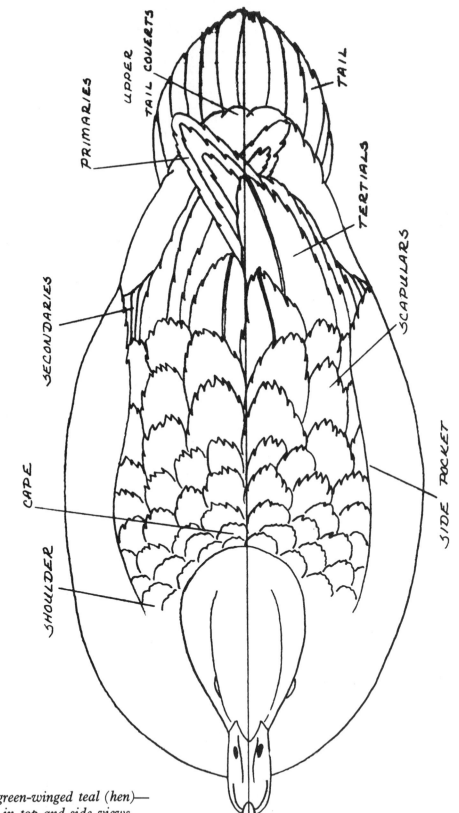

PRIMARIES

UPPER TAIL COVERTS

TAIL

TERTIALS

SECONDARIES

SCAPULARS

CAPE

SIDE POCKET

SHOULLDER

*Illus. 6. Anatomy of a green-winged teal (hen)—
a typical dabbler shown in top and side views.*

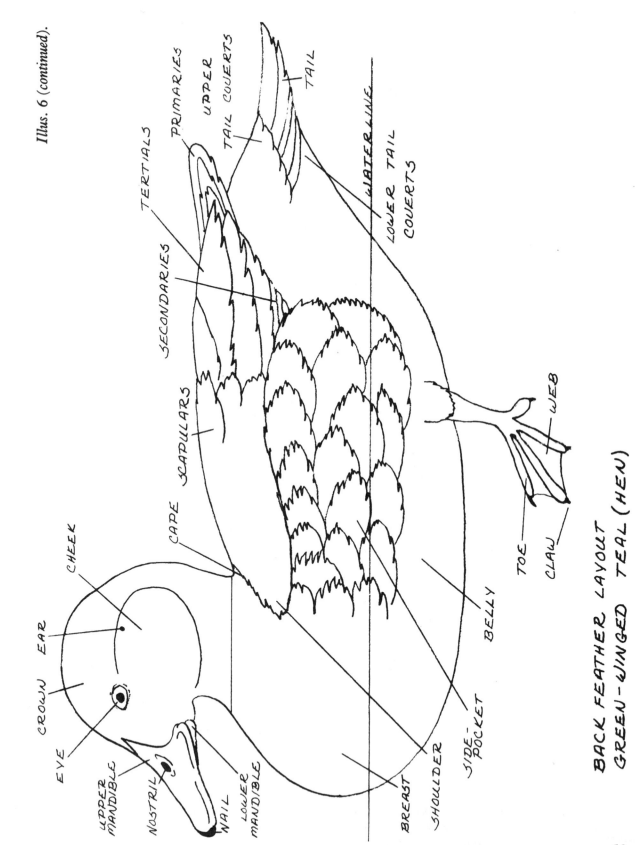

BACK FEATHER LAYOUT
GREEN-WINGED TEAL (HEN)

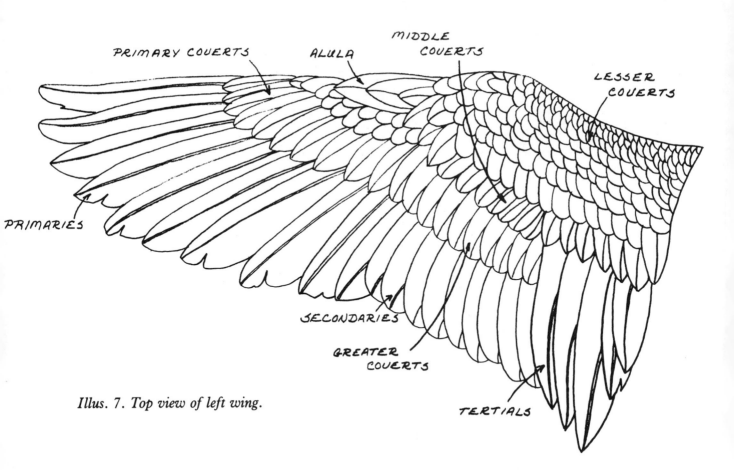

PRIMARY COVERTS ALULA MIDDLE COVERTS LESSER COVERTS

PRIMARIES

SECONDARIES

GREATER COVERTS

TERTIALS

Illus. 7. Top view of left wing.

There are, unfortunately, some exceptions to every rule that attempts to systemize nature. The wood duck, for example, doesn't fit a specific group. It is called a dabbler, but, technically, it is a perching duck because it nests in a tree. Another good example are the mergansers. They are usually grouped with divers but technically they should be in a class by themselves. Their exceptions to normal classifications will be explained later. The carver must know the major differences between each group: the subtle, little differences within a group from species to species as well as the differences between the males and females. A good, basic understanding of a duck's anatomy is obviously vitally important. Throughout this book you will be repeatedly reminded of the importance of studying the many aspects relating to the physical makeup of ducks. Study photos, mounts, skins, and best of all study live birds. An experienced carver expects and usually does find some small, quaint, little known or new quality about a particular species as he studies it in preparation for his next carving. And, of course, you need to know the anatomy so that your end result appears anatomically correct. Even though most ducks

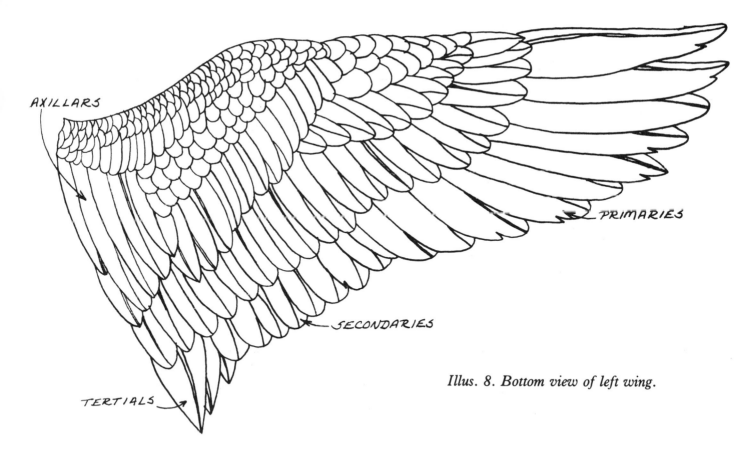

Illus. 8. Bottom view of left wing.

have the same basic parts and feather groups (Illus. 5–8), they are often shaped differently from one species to another. Let's look a little closer at some of the major differences between divers and dabblers.

Color. For the most part, dabblers are much more colorful birds than divers. Divers seem to have considerably more black and white on them whereas a dabbler's color range is vast and varies extremely from one species to another. This is especially true on the speculum area of the secondary wing feathers. See Illus. 5 and 6.

Wings (Illus. 7 and 8). The wings of diving ducks, though similar in structure, are smaller in relationship to the size of their bodies than those of dabbling ducks. This is why divers must run across the surface of the water in order to become airborne. Dabblers, on the other hand, can virtually leap out of the water to attain flight.

Feet (Illus. 9 and 10). The feet of a diver are much larger in relationship to its size and are set farther back on its body than are a

Illus. 9. Common mallard foot—a typical dabbler.

dabbler's. This allows a diver to propel itself much better under water. A diver also has a large lobe of skin on its hind toe which aids in its underwater mobility. With its feet set back, a diver takes on a much more erect stance when it is in the standing position.

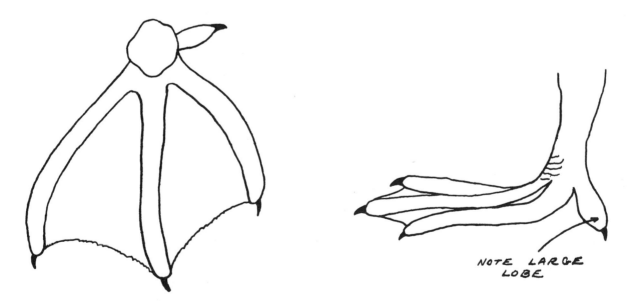

NOTE LARGE LOBE

Illus. 10. Canvasback foot—a typical diver.

Feathers. A diver's feathers tend to be shorter and broader than those of a dabbler. This is especially true on the scapular area and tertial area of most drakes. A dabbler's feathers in this area are longer and come to a point. They are almost spikelike in appearance. This also means that more shaft is exposed because of the longer feather. These feathers also take on more shape than a diver's feathers do. They tend to bend and curve around a duck's back. These variations are important to note when you are doing a carving. There are some exceptions to this rule, and we will deal with them in the chapter covering feather layout. Two very obvious differences are the wood duck and the hooded merganser. The wood duck, which is a dabbler, has almost square-shaped tertials. The hooded merganser's tertial feathers are the most spikelike of all and this duck is considered a diver.

There is also a difference in the smaller feathers, such as those of the breast area. The exposed area of these feathers on a diver seems to be broader and shorter. The hairs also seem to be straighter. On a dabbler, they tend to be a little more exposed, elongated, and the hairs are more curved and twisted. Giving attention to little details like these makes the difference between a good carving and a great one.

Tail feathers of divers are generally shorter and smaller than those of dabblers. Longer tail feathers aid flight maneuverability as do larger wings. This explains why dabblers are so graceful in flight, takeoffs, and landings, while divers tend to look much more awkward.

Bills (Illus. 11). The only group of ducks with distinctively different bills are the mergansers. Their long, pointed bills make excellent tools for fishing—their main source of food. This is where the obvious distinctions end. The bills of ducks are as variable as the species themselves and they encompass a wide range of colors. The other major distinction is in the shape of the nostril. A diver's nostril opening is long and narrow; a dabbler's nostril opening is shorter and wider. In some cases, the females' bills are smaller than the males'. Be sure to check your references to make sure the bill size is of the correct, proportionate size.

As you progress in the study of waterfowl, you will find more differences between divers and dabblers. Likewise, you will find exceptions to the usual rules. Those basic differences that have been briefly discussed here are intended to help the carver understand

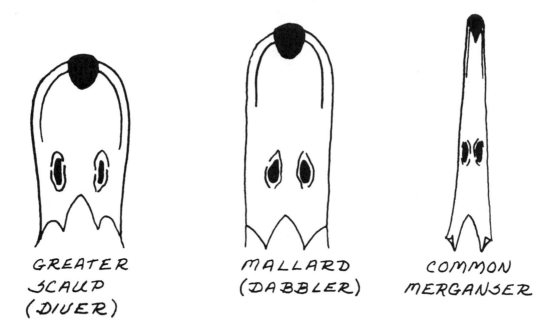

Illus. 11. Bill shapes from three different types of ducks.

basic duck anatomy. As you learn more and more about ducks, you will be alerted to many little details. Learn to look at individual feathers, rather than at the duck as a whole. A list grouping divers and dabblers is included here for your reference.

Divers

Canvasback	Old Squaw
Redhead	Common Merganser
Greater Scaup	Red-Breasted Merganser
Lesser Scaup	Hooded Merganser
Ring-Necked Duck	Bufflehead
Ruddy Duck	Common Goldeneye
Common Eider	Barrow's Goldeneye
King Eider	Black Scoter
Stellar's Eider	Surf Scoter
Spectacled Eider	Masked Duck
Harlequin Duck	

Dabblers

Gadwall

Mallard

Black Duck

Mottled Duck

Pintail

American Widgeon

European Widgeon

Green-Winged Teal

Blue-Winged Teal

Cinnamon Teal

Northern Shoveler

Wood Duck

AT REST

Illus. 12. Head of green-winged teal drake shown at resting position.

2. Capturing an Attitude

The key to creating a successful carving hinges on the carver's ability to capture a duck's particular attitude at a certain moment in its behavior. Like a human's, a duck's actions and movements have specific meanings. The changes in behavior sometimes happen quite quickly—as when suddenly frightened, or they are very gradual—as when a duck is resting or at ease.

In order to simplify and understand more easily the changes in appearance a duck has in accordance with its changes of attitude, it is necessary to recognize the basic areas of the duck that do change. One word of warning should be given here: Just like humans, ducks are not 100 percent consistent in their actions, and there are exceptions to every rule. The basic positions given in this chapter are the most common ones a duck goes through. There are many variations between those positions illustrated here that can also be achieved and represented in the completed carving.

EXCITED

Illus. 13. Same duck when excited or calling out. Note the rounded eye.

The Head

A duck's head is the most changeable part of the anatomy. It will set the tone of what particular attitude the carving is going to show. A duck's eye is the key to the head position.

Illus. 12 shows the head of a green-winged teal drake as it is resting. Very little of the neck is showing. The head is sunk down into the shoulders, which also pushes the breast area outward. The feathers along the crown of the head are in a very smooth and orderly state. The eye is about two-thirds open and quite oval in shape as the membrane around it is also quite relaxed.

Illus. 13 illustrates the same duck. Note how excited it looks—perhaps it is even calling out. The neck is extended and the feathers along the crown are quite ruffled. The eye is wide open and almost perfectly round as the membrane's muscles are tightened.

Illus. 14 shows a normal pose. This duck position is also somewhat alert, but it is not excited. His head is erect, and he is obviously paying attention to his surroundings. There is some rise to the feathers on the crown along the top of the head. Note that even though the duck is alert, the eye is not totally exposed. Except when excited, the eye always remains somewhat oval. Illus. 15 shows the typical sleeping pose. Again, the head sinks into the shoulders and the feathers

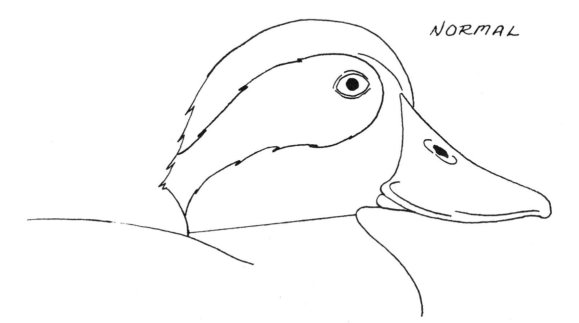

Illus. 14. The normal head position of an alert but not excited duck.

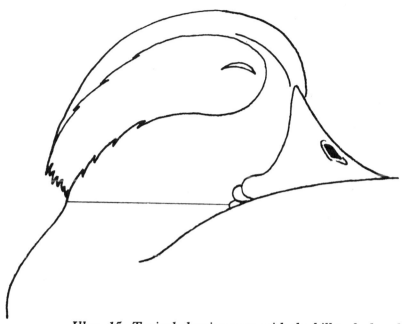

Illus. 15. Typical sleeping pose with the bill tucked under a wing.

along the crown are very smooth. In most such positions, the bill gets tucked under a wing and the eye is closed. It is important to note that the membrane covering the eye comes up from the bottom and not down from the top.

The Crest

Some species of ducks have crests. The most noted of these are the wood ducks and the hooded mergansers. Their crests are things of beauty and very changeable at different times. When the wood duck is alert, as in Illus. 16, the crest is raised and no part of it touches the duck's back. The aft tip of the crest almost comes to a point when the duck is in this alert position. Illus. 17 shows a wood duck at rest. As mentioned before, the head sinks into the shoulders and very little, if any, of the neck is exposed. The crest feathers lie down on the back of the bird and fan out. This means that the aft tip of the crest no longer comes to a point as it does in Illus. 16. The appropriate "attitude" detail should be evident in your carving. (See Illus. 17.)

The other time that crests are in various positions is during mating. The best way to see what a duck's head does when he is mating, is to actually witness this spectacle. Individual poses of this process are illustrated in the *Decoy Pattern Book* (Sterling Publishing Co., forthcoming) by Keith Bridenhagen. When a duck is mating, the poses

Illus. 16. A wood duck with head erect.
Note the pointed aft of the crest.

change rapidly from second to second. It would be to every carver's benefit to witness this activity in person, at a zoo, in a wildlife sanctuary, or in the wild. It is truly an unforgettable experience.

Primary Feathers and Tail Area

The other main areas of concern a carver has to deal with are the primary wing feathers and the area of the tail.

Illus. 18 shows a duck with its primaries crossed and the tail

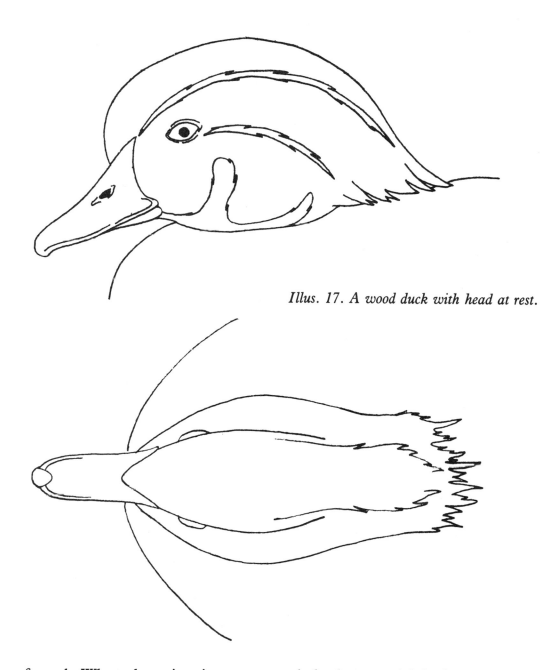

Illus. 17. A wood duck with head at rest.

fanned. When the primaries are crossed the large tertial feathers overlap and less of the wing slips down into the side-pocket area. Crossed primaries generally point in an upward direction. The fanned tail rides low in the water and usually means some sort of action is taking place. Either the duck is ready for flight, using the tail for a rudder to turn in the water, or it is just drying its feathers. There is no one center feather to the tail. There are, in fact, two sides to the tail which show up well when the tail is fanned. Note in Illus. 18 that a fanned tail has exposed shafts on its feathers.

Illus. 19 shows a duck with its primaries open and the tail closed.

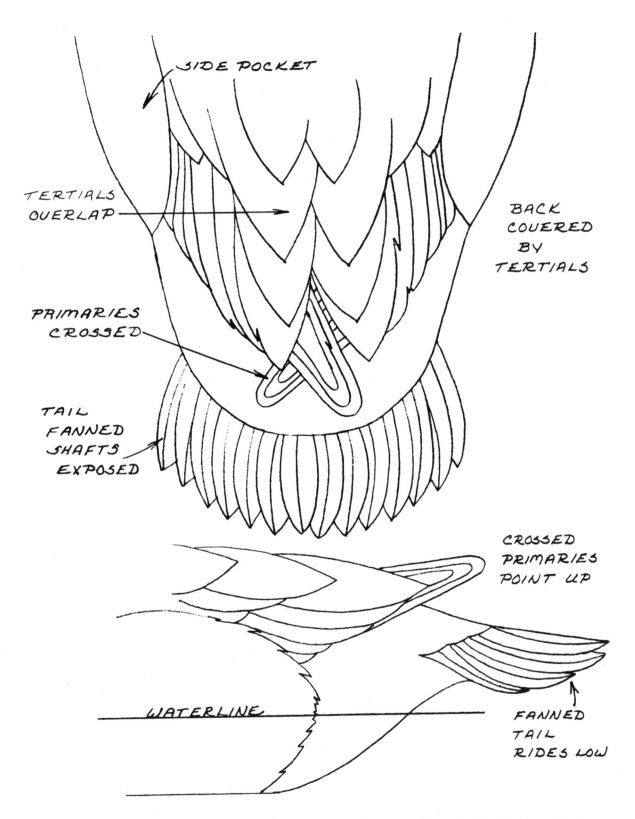

SIDE POCKET

TERTIALS OVERLAP

BACK COVERED BY TERTIALS

PRIMARIES CROSSED

TAIL FANNED SHAFTS EXPOSED

CROSSED PRIMARIES POINT UP

WATERLINE

FANNED TAIL RIDES LOW

Illus. 18. Fanned tail with crossed primaries.

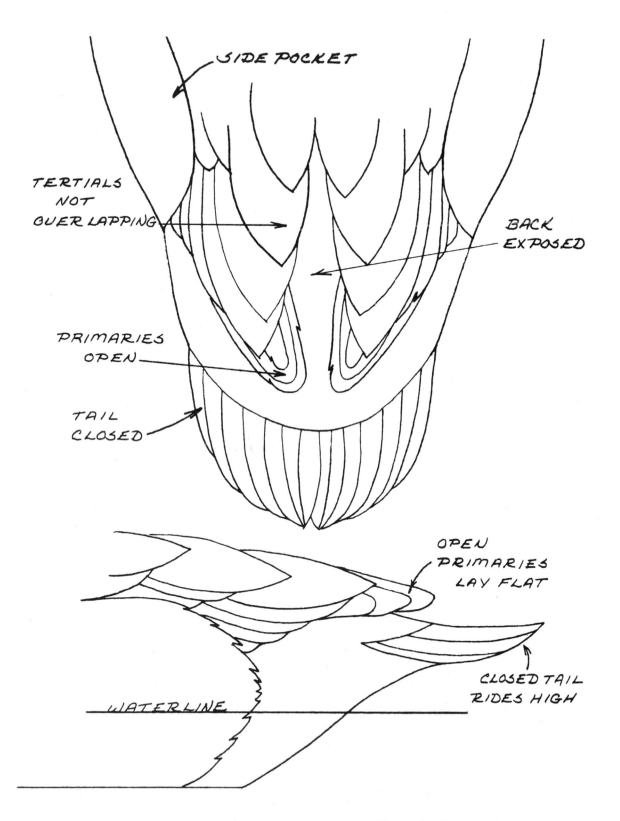

SIDE POCKET

TERTIALS NOT OVERLAPPING

BACK EXPOSED

PRIMARIES OPEN

TAIL CLOSED

OPEN PRIMARIES LAY FLAT

CLOSED TAIL RIDES HIGH

WATERLINE

Illus. 19. Closed tail with open primaries.

Open primaries expose much of the back area and allow more of the wing to slip into the side-pocket area. If the back is exposed, the tertial feathers no longer overlap. Instead, they are in separate groups with each wing. An open primary also tends to lie flatter along a duck's back.

The closed tail generally points in an upward direction. A closed tail is more evident when a duck is at rest. A closed tail gives the illusion of a central tail feather but, as mentioned, this is not the case. The only shaft that is exposed on a closed tail is what appears to be the central feather. The other feathers overlap in such a way that their shafts are not exposed.

These two examples of primaries and tails (as shown in Illus. 18 and 19), unfortunately, are not always the rule. Just because the primaries are crossed, a tail does not have to be fanned. A good carver will use his imagination and take the various aspects of the entire anatomy into account to determine exactly how to "pose" his work.

Feathers

Feathers also can indicate a different appearance at different phases of a duck's attitude. We have already seen how the feathers of a duck's head can change from being at rest to being excited. This fact holds true as well for the entire anatomy. Sometimes feathers can look all puffy—at other times the feathers can appear to be all matted down.

Illus. 20. A dry feather looks full and puffy.

Illus. 21. Wet feathers will change the appearance dramatically.

This feature changes according to the amount of oil a duck has on its feathers, the muscular contraction it makes and whether feathers are wet or dry. (See Illus. 20 and 21.) Making feathers look wet and matted on the side-pocket area of a carving can change its look quite radically.

The best way to observe these special details is to study live specimens. Visit a zoo or rookery (breeding ground). All the drawings, photos, and mounted specimens in the world cannot give you the precise realism that comes from actually seeing a real, live duck going through its motions.

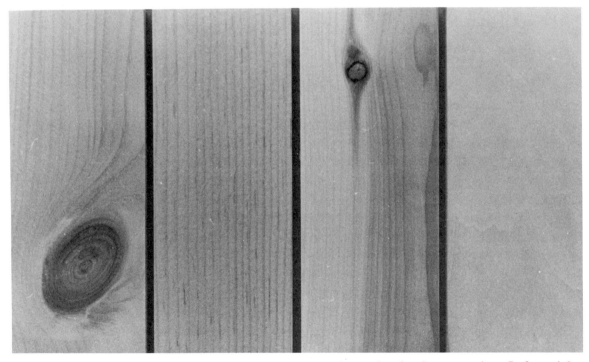

Illus. 22. Time-tested woods still popular for decoy carving. Left to right: Northern white pine, sugar pine, white cedar, and basswood.

3. Wood Selection

This chapter gives a brief overview of some of the current and popular choices of woods used by professional decoy carvers. Selecting a block of wood to match your carving needs and expectations is a very important matter and should not be dealt with lightly. Among your considerations are factors pertaining to availability, cost, and quality. The wood must be the best possible choice for the job at hand. Refer to *Making Wood Decoys* (Patrick Spielman, Sterling Publishing Co., New York, 1982) for basic information about drying and laminating chunks of wood in suitable sizes for decoys along with some alternative ideas for conditioning carving materials.

White Pine (Illus. 22). This easy-to-carve wood has been used for many years to make hunting decoys. It can often be purchased in large blocks at a fairly reasonable price. Today, many pre-carved decoy kits come in white pine. A higher grade, clear piece is best for a textured carving.

Its grain does show through somewhat when it is burned and the pitch will leave some residue on burning tools. White pine, containing one or more knots, will make an excellent natural finished carving and a beautiful decorative piece. It can also be stained various colors to match or contrast with surroundings if desired.

Sugar Pine (Illus. 22). This wood can make beautiful textured carvings if it can be located with small tight grain lines. Finding large pieces of it is not easy. Usually it is best to purchase 2-inch stock and glue-laminate it to make larger pieces. Good sugar pine is fairly expensive and in some areas may be difficult to obtain. It carves, textures, and burns exceptionally well, but it does leave some residue on burning tips because of its pitch content. Clear sugar pine generally has uninteresting grain or figure patterns. For this reason it is seldom used for the natural finished carving, unless it contains some knots or other interesting features.

White Cedar (Illus. 22). The traditional wood, used by old-time decoy makers, which has withstood the test of time, and which has a century-old reputation for making excellent, lightweight and durable hunting decoys. In some areas of the United States it may be available at lumberyards or carving-supply centers. Its cost is relatively low and in areas where it grows locally it is (comparatively) the least expensive of decoy-carving woods. If one can find a clear piece with few knots, it will make an excellent feather-carved bird. It is very easy to carve with a knife or power tools and sands to a nice smooth surface. If it has any drawback at all, it is that sometimes its grain or growth ring patterns show through when it is burned. (See Illus. 23.) This condition, though acceptable for functional, working decoys, is not highly desirable in the detailed, textured, and realistic, or competition decoy. The better woods for carving such decoys have more uniformity in their density throughout. In other words, the hardness of the summer and spring growth areas of the annual ring are essentially the same. When using woods that vary in hardness in the growth rings, such as cedar so often does, it is best to use a coarser form of texture carving prior to burning. Incidentally, a piece of knotty cedar can make a beautiful natural-finished carving and it takes stains fairly well too.

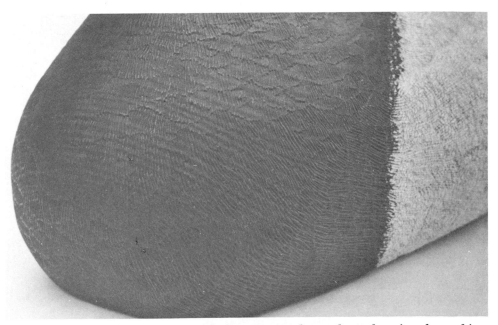

Illus. 23. A close look at this breast area shows the end-grain telegraphing of the wood growth rings through the textured, burned, and painted surface. Avoid woods with alternating hard and soft growth rings to eliminate this less than desirable situation.

Basswood or Linden (Illus. 22). Here is a clear white wood that makes excellent textured carvings. It seems almost totally to lack grain or figure. It is one of the traditionally good carving woods because it has that uniformity of density as discussed. Basswood can be found in large chunks at rural sawmills. It can also be purchased in chunks specifically cut and seasoned for decoy carving from mail-order sources. Should you intend to cut your own wood, it is best cut in the winter when the sap is down in the tree. This reduces the drying time a great deal. Wood should be dried slowly in a place where changes in temperature are very gradual.

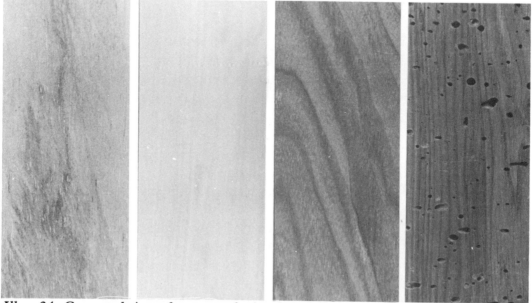

Illus. 24. Current choices of many professionals include left to right: Jelutong (from Malaya) and tupelo (from swamp lands in the southeastern United States) for highly detailed, textured, and painted carvings. Clear butternut and wormy butternut among other beautiful woods are used for decoys with natural, transparent finishes.

If basswood has any drawback at all, it is that it tends to "fuzz" when worked with power tools. Some extra sanding will be necessary to eliminate this minor problem. Basswood burns cleanly with very little residue and its grain does not telegraph or show through the painted carving at all. The value of basswood for natural-finished birds is low as it lacks the grain pattern or figure found in many other choices of beautiful woods.

Jelutong (Illus. 24). This tropical wood can be carved beautifully with knife and power tool. Its lack of visible grain lines makes for great textured and painted carvings without any "show through" at all. It tends to "fuzz" slightly but this is easily overcome with a little extra sanding. One of its major disadvantages is its higher cost.

It has not been easy to obtain. A number of the top carvers have gone to great trouble to get it and have paid well for it. Because it has excellent carving qualities and is in demand, this unusual wood is becoming easier to obtain from the increasing number of mail-order sources that handle it. Jelutong usually is not available in thick dimensions; thus pieces must be laminated together to make a suitable size block. This along with its uninteresting figure pattern makes it less than desirable for decoys that are to be made with natural transparent finishes.

Tupelo (Illus. 24). A very white and seemingly grainless wood, it grows in the southern swamplands of the United States. As a realistic decoy-carving material, it is (as of recent years) the highest regarded and most sought-after wood among reputable carvers. A special feature is that it can be purchased in very large one-piece sizes. This allows carvers to make solid decoy bodies without gluing or laminating smaller pieces together. It dries to a desirable lightweight, easily worked material with little evidence of checking or splitting as is common to most other woods when dried in sufficient thicknesses.

Tupelo carves like butter when you wet the surface and if you leave it dry, it works up beautifully with power tools regardless of grain direction. Feather carving and detailing is very easy with tupelo, because it doesn't "fuzz." It burns very cleanly. The wood is exceptionally buoyant. Painting it seems to draw the paint into its surface even after some sealer is applied. Tupelo is fairly expensive, but this cost is far overshadowed by the great end results achieved with minimal carving problems. Tupelo is not at all recommended for decoys having clear, natural-wood finishes. As a wood, it is totally boring and uninteresting visually, but for carving detailed, textured, and painted decoys it has no equal.

Butternut (Illus. 24 and 25). This northern grown wood, is in our opinion, the most beautiful of any wood to use for natural-finished decoys. It is not recommended for textured decoys that will be painted. Butternut is every bit as pretty as walnut and it is much easier to carve. Its look has a very special appeal suggesting a visual softness appropriate to a decoy carving that is unsurpassed by any other wood. A unique feature of butternut is that it can be found in the wood lot with varying degrees of soundness and looks. It may be found "wormy" which not only has beautiful grain, but also the small wormholes that add even more visual impact and interest. If you are fortunate and find good sources for butternut, you will enjoy carving it. The results will be more than charming—guaranteed. Refer to chapter 13 for more illustrations of butternut worked into decoys with natural transparent finishes.

Illus. 25. This close-up shows the unique features of butternut grain. Its special pattern and figure make butternut very desirable for decoys with natural finishes.

Laminating. As we know, laminating is often the only solution one has to acquire a block of sufficient size to carve a decoy. There are some carvers who prefer the lamination method to working with solid, one-piece blocks. This includes those carvers who make their decoys with hollow bodies. Hollowing is a technique used by some carvers to achieve special qualities of buoyancy; they also feel that removing the "inside" reduces stresses in the wood that might cause cracks to appear. Refer to *Making Wood Decoys* (Patrick Spielman, Sterling Publishing Co., New York, 1982) which highlights the essential differences between solid body and laminated or hollow-body decoy construction.

Any time you laminate you are creating a potential flaw in the carving. Even making the head from a separate piece and gluing it to the body is a form of laminating. There are two basic ways of laminating a decoy body block, that is, so that the glue lines run either horizontally or vertically. (See Illus. 26.) Some carvers feel that the vertical method is best and still others prefer to glue pieces horizontally—one on top of another. In either case, try to plan the glue lines so that they come out in inconspicuous places such as under wings and under tails.

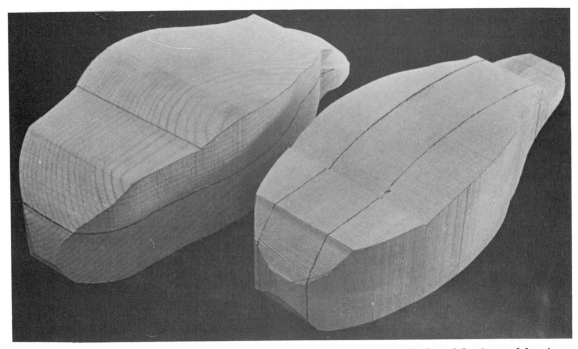

Illus. 26. Built-up decoy bodies showing vertical and horizontal laminations.

In laminating there are several other important considerations. First, if you must laminate, a tight fit and thin glue lines are essential. Second, remember that with every different piece of wood entered into the laminated block, you are entering a new variable into your work piece. Since no two pieces of wood are ever exactly alike they may expand or shrink at different rates. This will eventually cause the various layers to become visible at the glue line. The best precaution against this is to laminate pieces of wood that are: (1) of the same species, (2) cut from the same board or cut from the same part of the tree, and (3) are of the same moisture content. Remember that each individual piece of wood has its own performance qualities depending on how it was cut from the tree. It has its own grain patterns, its own contained stresses, and, consequently, its own rates and directions of dimensional movements in expansion or contraction.

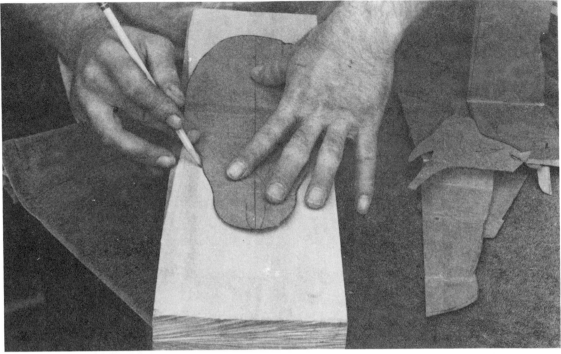

Illus. 27. Laying out the top-view pattern.

Illus. 28. Laying out the side-view pattern.

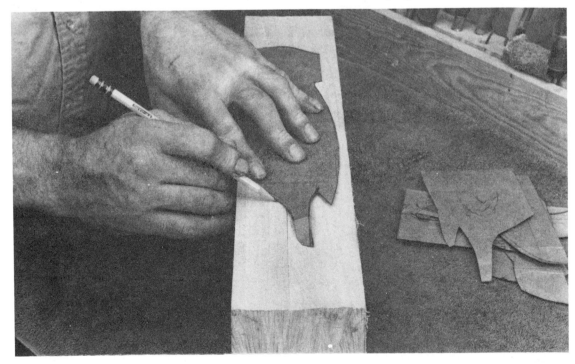

4. Basic Steps to a Smooth Carving

Before we can get into laying out, carving, and texturing feathers, we need to have a properly shaped carving with smooth surfaces. This chapter highlights some of the basic steps involved to accomplish this. If necessary, refer to *Making Wood Decoys* (Patrick Spielman, Sterling Publishing Co., New York, 1982) which gives all of the essential step-by-step instructions involved in shaping and smoothing a carving.

Illus. 27 to 29 illustrate laying out the body pattern on the squared, rough block. Using a block that has been squared helps you to achieve an evenly proportioned cutout on both sides of the center line. This also helps to balance the carving later.

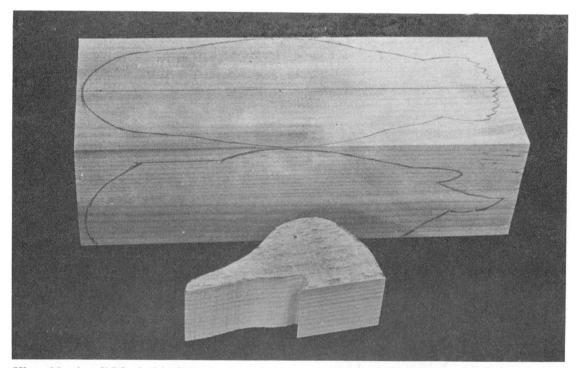

Illus. 29. A solid body block laid out ready for sawing. The head profile is already cut out from 2-inch stock.

Illus. 30. Band-sawing the top-view profile. Note: *Saw the body shape by starting the cuts from each end, leaving it partially uncut near the center. This technique keeps the waste pieces intact for the next step.*

Illus. 30 and 31 show band-sawing the top and side views of the block. Notice that when sawing the top view, we start cuts from both ends of the block, and leave it partially uncut in the middle. This makes cutting the side profile considerably safer (Illus. 31).

A typical sawn-out block and head are shown in Illus. 32. The head has been cut out from a piece of 2-inch material. The excess wood

Illus. 31. Sawing the side-view profile.

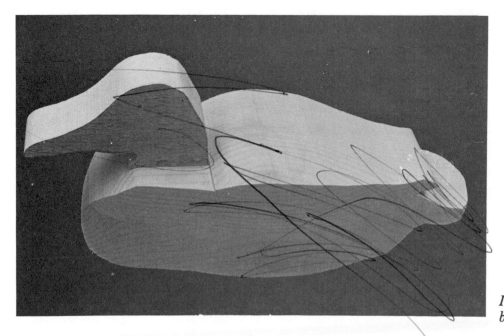

Illus. 32. The sawn-out block and head.

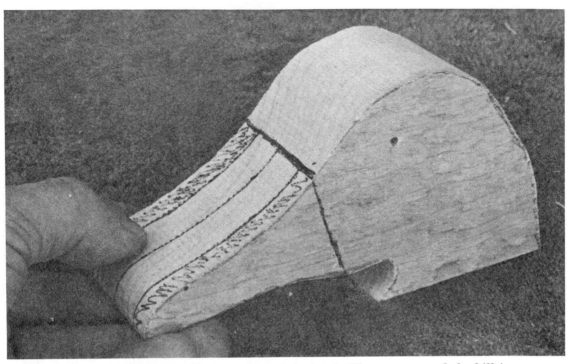

Illus. 33. Closeup view of the head. The area around the bill is cut away with a coping saw.

Illus. 34. Blocks with rough shaping started.

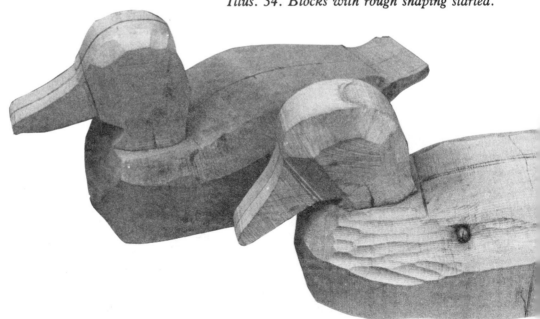

Illus. 35. Use whatever tooling works best for you (such as this rotary bit), to achieve the final shape.

around the bill area (Illus. 33), can be removed by hand, using a coping saw or other suitable tool. Rough shaping (which has been started in Illus. 34) can be done with a wide variety of hand tools such as chisels, gouges, hatchets, and drawknives. Many carvers prefer the use of flexible-shaft power tools as shown in Illus. 35. Refer to chapter 15 for more information about tools and cutters.

Once the body has been pretty well worked to a basic rough shape, rough carve the head. After this has been achieved, check the fit between the head and the body (Illus. 36). Establish the head's location and position with a reference mark. Some carvers use a dowel to join the head and body together as shown in Illus. 37. This adds strength to the joint and is an absolute must in hunting decoys which are often handled roughly. Some carvers just glue the head directly to the body without a dowel as in Illus. 38. This is acceptable with decorative decoys which are handled more carefully.

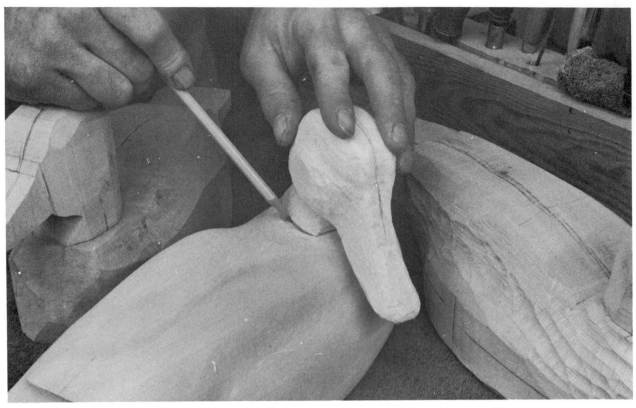

Illus. 36. Locating the position of the head.

Illus. 37. Securing the head with a dowel.

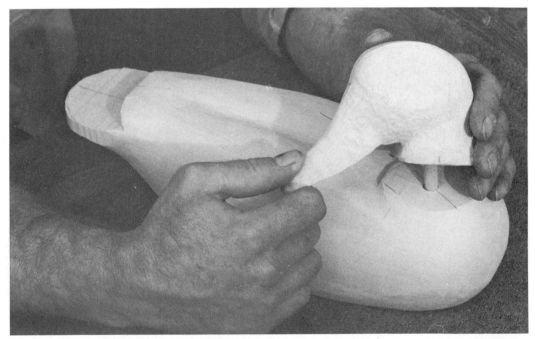

Illus. 38. Some heads are simply glued on as shown here with this kit decoy.

Some carvers prefer to attach the head before any shaping is done. Others prefer to carve it completely (Illus. 39), before it is attached. Some even go as far as to finish carving and then paint every detail on the head before joining it to the body.

Illus. 39. An optional step. Some carvers prefer to finish carving the head before gluing it to the body.

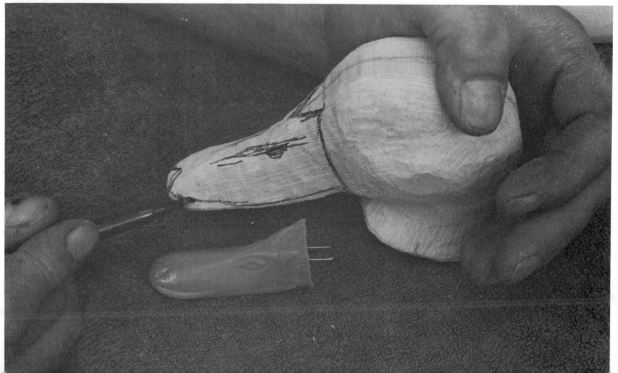

Illus. 40. Precarved kits are available in many popular species for those who have limited work space, tools, or limited access to raw materials.

Illus. 41. This precarved canvasback kit comes rough-carved to shape, as shown here, along with the eyes on wire.

Kits (Illus. 40–42). Many varieties of decoy kits are available in most species of ducks. If one does not have an adequate work space, ample equipment or the availability of raw materials, consideration should be given to working with kits. Kits can often be reworked to a new or desired shape. They can also be textured and realistically detailed. A simple knife, a burning tool, and finish or paint is all that's necessary to create a decoy to your liking. Using kits is also a good way to try your hand at decoy carving without investing in a lot of time or money.

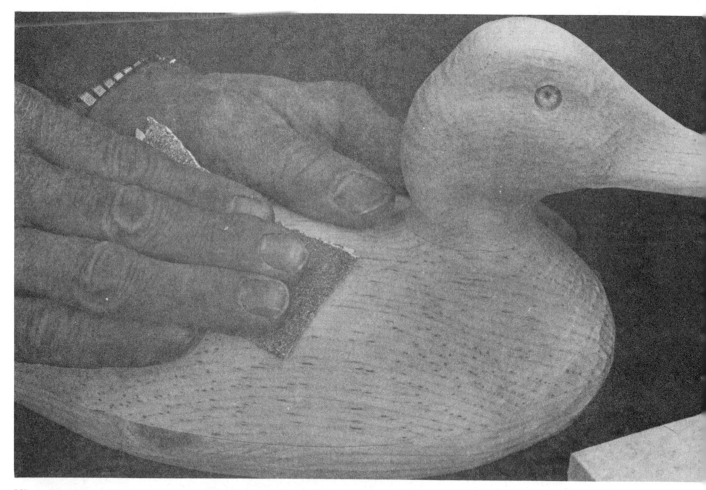

Illus. 42. Most kits require no more than final sanding.

Most advanced carvers, however, start their carvings directly from the raw block. Thus, they are in complete control of every phase of the carving. They know and understand the qualities of their material as well as its limits.

Smoothing the Surface. A very smooth surface is essential for an accurate feather layout, with the actual detailing to come later. To attain a very smooth surface, sand with progressively finer grits, ending with a fine abrasive such as 150 grit. In order to eliminate pesty fibres and raised grain, use the "denatured alcohol trick." Since denatured alcohol dries almost instantly, it is more desirable than water for raising grain fibres. Water will achieve the same results but it soaks into the wood and the surfaces dry much slower. A light application of the denatured alcohol over the wood surface will raise the grain fibres. Do a final sanding with 180- or 220-grit paper; this makes for a "super smooth" surface. (See Illus. 43.) The denatured alcohol can be applied lightly with a rag or sprayed on in mist form with an atomizer. An expensive atomizer is not necessary for this procedure. A discarded spray deodorant container or an empty perfume applicator will do nicely. One application of alcohol mist is usually sufficient, but you may want to repeat the procedure on the end grain areas. The breast area and where extra smoothness is desired (such as the bill) may need more than one application followed again by fine sanding.

Illus. 43. After sanding, coat the surface with denatured alcohol. Apply with rag or atomizer, let dry and sand again to get a very smooth surface.

Now that the surface has been finely sanded, the decoy is ready for: (1) an application of a natural finish, (2) a paint job, or (3) feather texturing or other carving details. This obviously would be the stopping point if one were doing a naturally finished decoy made of butternut, walnut, or some other finely patterned wood. Let's not forget, however, that some advanced detailing techniques can be carved on naturally finished carvings. Some of these ideas will be dealt with in other chapters.

Whatever type of carving you are working on, a surface that is smooth is an essential step in the progression towards the finished bird.

Since many carvers like to finally shape the head before it is attached to the body, the next chapter will cover "head details."

Illus. 44. The head of a mallard drake completely finished with detailed carving and realistic painting. Obviously, precise proportions and attention to detail is essential to achieve reality.

5. Head Details

All of the individual areas of the head must be worked carefully so that when viewed all together the result will be of the right proportions typical of a good looking, realistic carving (Illus. 44). The area of the most exacting requirements is the bill, which does not change in dimension once a duck has reached maturity. The bill must be carved to exact shape and size. The authenticity of the entire carving hinges on the bill's dimensions. Some carvers purchase study bills (made of cast plastic). They are available in almost every species of duck (Illus. 45). Real bills (Illus. 46), can also be used as a good reference for details.

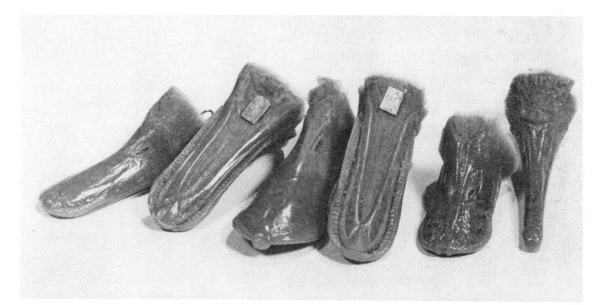

Illus. 45. Study bills made of cast plastic are available for most species. Photo courtesy of Oscar Johnston Wildlife Gallery.

It is important to remember that bills shrink almost immediately after a duck has been killed. This is especially true at the base where the bill meets the head. When using study bills, look for signs of shrinkage, and shrivelling marks and take this into consideration when judging the bill's size for accuracy. If you are using real bills, remember that the color also fades almost immediately. It's best to check other kinds of reference materials to obtain the truest colors.

In the chapter on anatomy, it was pointed out that the nostril areas of divers and dabblers were shaped differently. Regardless of size, all nostrils are relieved so that they have a ridge surrounding the opening

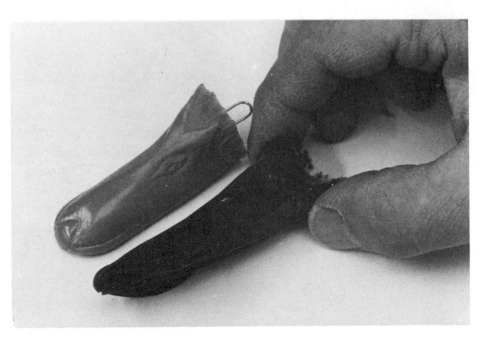

Illus. 46. Real bills (lower one) can also be used as good visual references.

(Illus. 47). On realistic carvings, the opening goes all the way through the bill; thus, if you look at the nostril from the right angle, you can see light through the bill (Illus. 48).

Illus. 47. Relieving the area around the nostril.

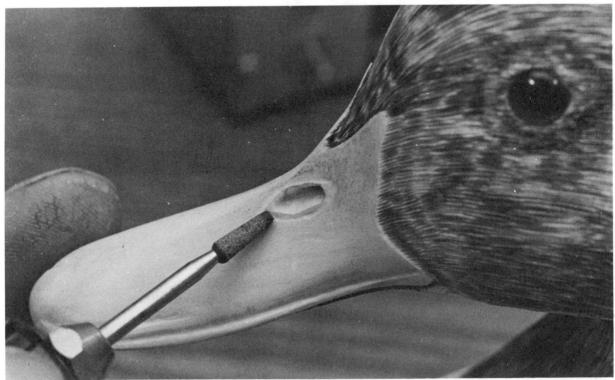

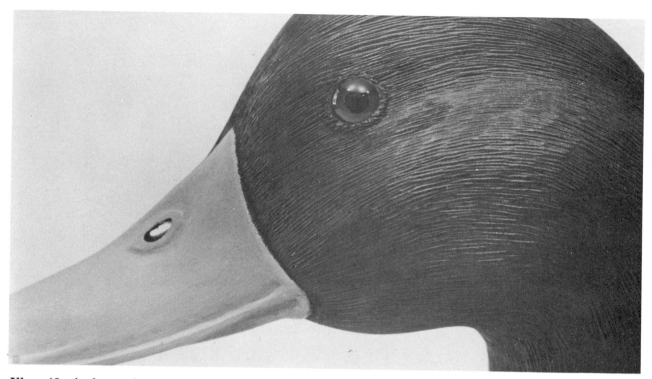

Illus. 48. A closeup look at the finished nostril and eye details. Note that the nostril opening goes completely through the bill.

Illus. 49. Laying out contours on the underside of the bill.

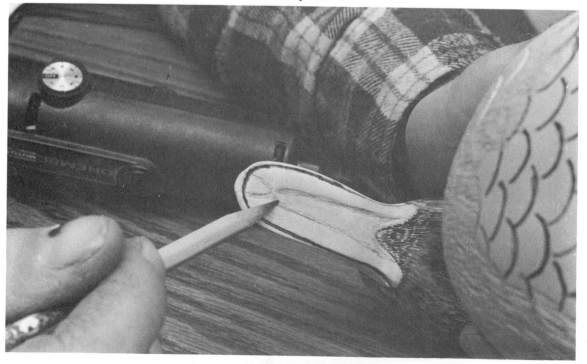

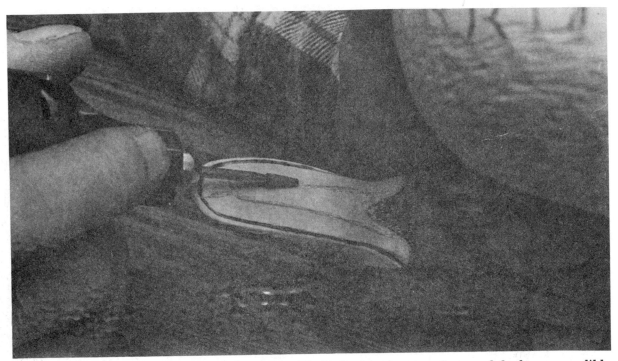

Illus. 50. Relieving the central area of the lower mandible.

Illus. 51. Working the nail area in slight relief.

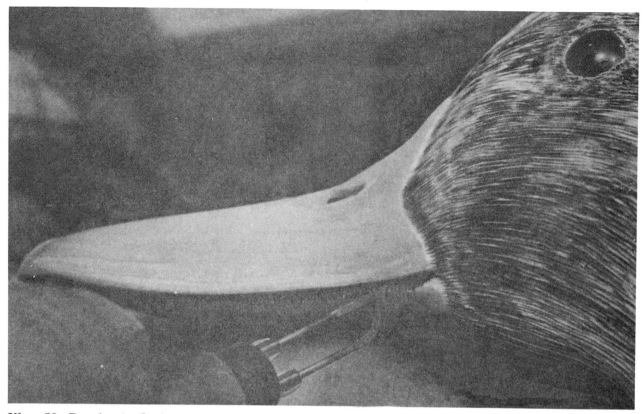

Illus. 52. Burning in the lamellae.

The lower mandible of a bill (Illus. 49) has as much detail as the upper mandible, and the obvious details certainly should not be overlooked. Most details on the lower mandible can be carved with a fine grinding stone (Illus. 50). The contour details are slight and some sanding is required. The lower half of the bill has a nail (Illus. 51) nearly like the upper half. It is not as prominent on the lower half, but it is just as essential in the duck's anatomy.

Another important detail on the bill is the lamellae. These are the duck's fine water-straining devices and they can best be detailed by burning each individual one on both the upper and the lower mandible. (See Illus. 52.)

With the bill completely carved, as shown in Illus. 53, several coats of sealer should be applied with sanding between each coat. This gives the bill hardness as well as a really smooth finish (Illus. 54).

Illus. 54 also shows the eye already set in and filled with putty. This

Illus. 53. The top and side views of this pintail bill, as finished carved, show the nostril nail and other highlights.

is the area to carve and texture next. The eye is another area of great importance on a carving, because it draws one's visual attention to the carving. There are many sources for glass eyes. Some sources are listed in the Appendix.

Carve an eyelid area around the eye (Illus. 55). This ridge around the eye must be made to look more subtle and not too prominent.

Illus. 54. Sealing the bill. Apply several coats, if necessary, sanding in between coats to harden the bill. Note how the eye on this decoy has been set into place with wood filler.

Illus. 55. Carving the eyelid.

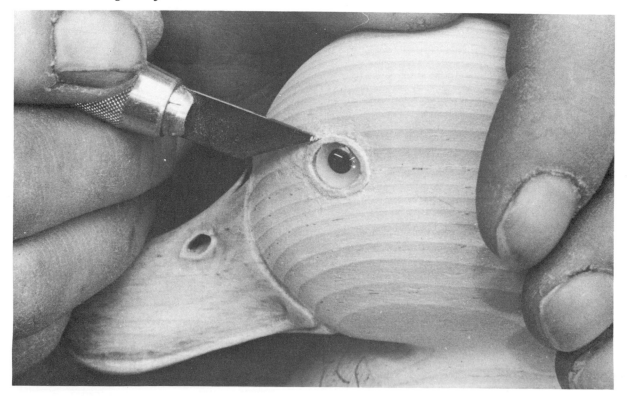

Illus. 56. Burning the raised area around the eye to form an eyelid.

Illus. 57. Observing an actual duck head helps to determine the look of real feather structures. Detailing practice is started on a scrap block.

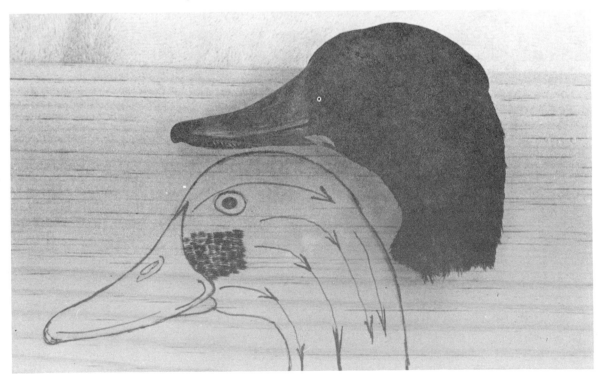

Illus. 58. This closeup look shows the series of short, irregular burning strokes that simulate the real textured look.

This is best done by burning down the eyelid using low heat (Illus. 56). This way you can slowly cut down on the size of the lid and texture it at the same time without harming the glass eye as would sandpaper or a grinding stone. Remember to be concerned about the look of your carving's attitude here. Make the eye show the duck's behavior as discussed in the chapter on attitudes.

Before starting to feather-texture the head, some serious study must be given to the head's hairlike feathers and how they are structured. Studying actual duck heads (Illus. 57) is an excellent exercise. Upon close examination, you will notice these feathers are essentially a series of short hairs all blended together. Each feather shows no definite beginning or end. Do the burning to imitate this look. Use short irregular strokes, and try not to develop a rigid or set pattern (Illus. 58). Practice burning these strokes on some scrap pieces of wood to perfect the techniques before actually burning the feather strokes on the carving itself.

The logical place to start burning is at the base of the bill (Illus. 59). Try to think of a duck as the roof of a house. Starting at the base of the bill, the feathers all lap over one another all the way to the tail,

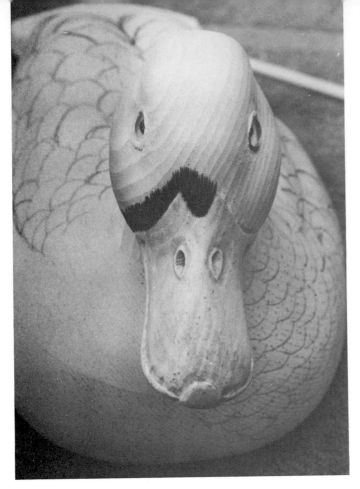

Illus. 59. Feather burning is started at the bill and continues toward the neck.

Illus. 60. As burning continues some touch-up work may be necessary around the eyes.

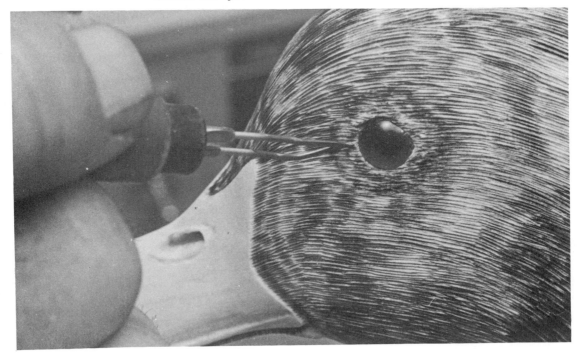

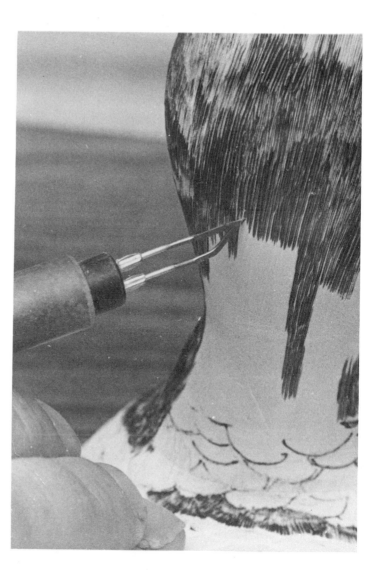

Illus. 61. Feather strokes become longer and deeper as you work down the neck. The lower neck is the blending area for the cape and breast feathers.

as do the shingles on a roof. As you continue work on the head, you may see the need to do some touching up and blending where the eyelids meet the short, irregular strokes on the head (Illus. 60). The farther down the head, the larger the feathers. Your strokes gradually become longer and deeper to effect that appearance (Illus. 61).

Some carvers fine-grind the lower head area with a fine stone to give it a more textured appearance before burning. This is often done to represent an excited bird where the feathers on the top of the head and the back of the neck appear somewhat ruffled. This is also done on the crest areas where the feathers are quite a bit larger. While burning the neck area, begin to think about blending these hairlike feathers into the larger feathers of the shoulder, breast, and cape areas. The next chapter deals with feather groups, how to make individual feathers, and how to blend the different areas together.

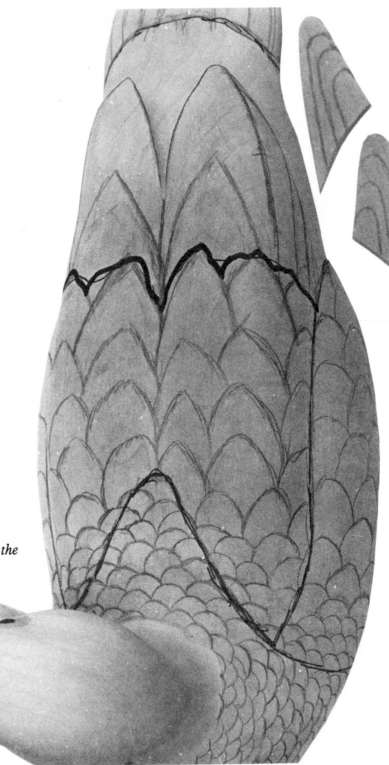

Illus. 62. A general top view of the common feather groups.

6. Feather Layout and Detailing

In addition to the feathers of the head and neck, the other areas of a duck's feathers can be categorized according to major groups. Illus. 62 and 63 show the essential feather groups separated with bold, dark lines. The individual primary inserts are also shown, but these will be dealt with in the next chapter.

The use of a mount (Illus. 64) can be helpful in several ways. First of all, individual feathers can be selected from it and studied. Secondly, the mount shows how each feather group or area of feathers coincide and blend with the feather area next to it.

Illus. 63. A general side view of the common feather groups.

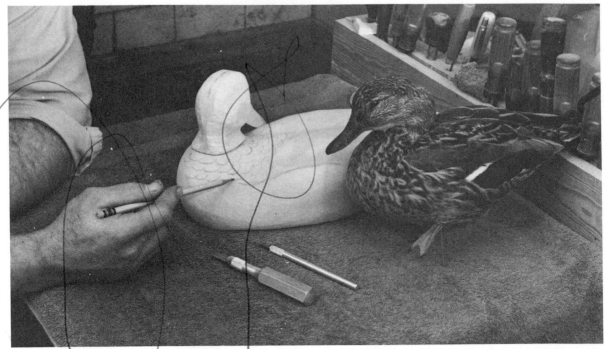

Illus. 64. Using a mount (or stuffed) bird as an aid in laying out the various feather groups.

Illus. 65. View of a finished mallard drake decoy, which shows the secondary feather group (in the central area of the photo). This area is where five different feather groups merge.

Greater scaup drake (bluebill).

A

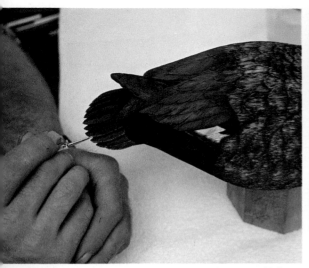

Making the edges of the tail feathers lighter.

Applying initial wash coat to scapular area.

Highlighting various shades of green on head.

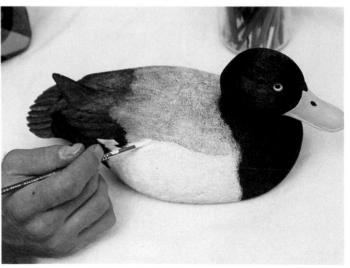

Adding final light washes over vermiculated side-pocket area.

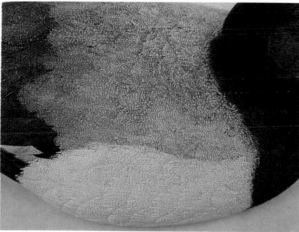

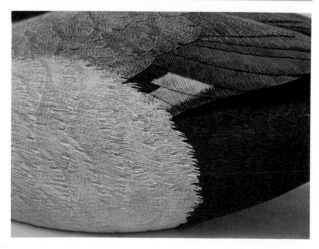

(Top) Close-up of head details.

(Upper left) Top view of cape and scapular areas.

(Right) Top view of tertials, inserted primaries, and tail.

(Left) Rear side-pocket area and secondary feather group.

C

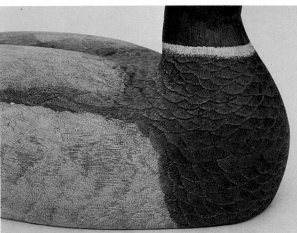

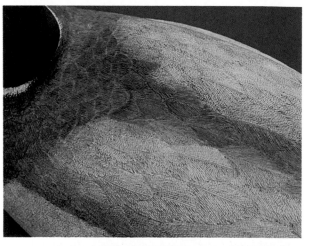

(Top right) *The popular mallard drake.*

(Above left) *Side view showing neck, breast, and shoulder area.*

(Above right) *Top view showing cape and scapular area.*

(Right) *Close-up showing inserted primaries, oil-gland coverts, and the tail.*

D

(Top) The red-breasted merganser drake.

(Left) Head and breast area.

*(Right) Detail showing open primaries, secondaries, and
side-pocket area.*

(Top) The canvasback drake on base with poured plastic over rocks.

(Above left) Side view.

(Above right) Profile of head and bill.

(Left) Rear top view showing inserted primaries and tail.

Goldeneye drake with inserted primaries.

Ruddy duck hen.

Bluebill in natural butternut.

Top view of ruddy duck, showing back and fanned tail.

G

(Right) The common loon in butternut.

(Right) The hooded merganser drake in wormy butternut.

(Above) Wing of blue-winged teal.

(Right) Blue-winged teal in butternut.

H

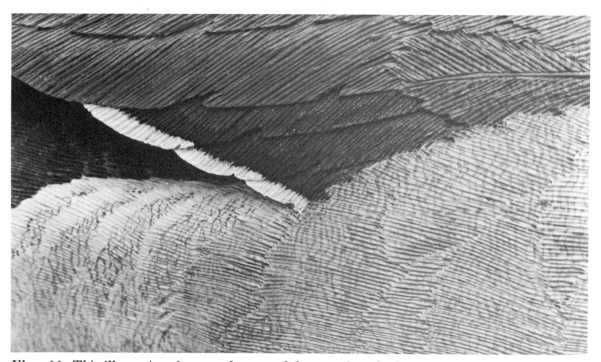

Illus. 66. This illustration shows a close-up of the secondary feathers or speculum area.

Illus. 65 shows a view from a completed mallard drake carving where five different feather groups merge. This photo is worthy of careful study. Illus. 66 shows the same area but isolates the secondary feathers with a good deal of magnification. This example of very carefully isolating and studying specific feathers must be employed to reproduce the individual detailing feather by feather over the entire body of the duck. At the same time, the individual feather must always relate to others in its group in proportion, size, and shape. Totally, its group must relate correctly to the other groups surrounding it. A practice board will be a valuable learning and skill-developing exercise. Practice drawing out a secondary feather group and isolate one feather. Illus. 67 through 72 illustrate the essential steps in producing one feather in this group. Now you can refer to the photos showing the secondary group on the finished mallard. See how your carved and burned feather compares to it. Once satisfied with your own skills in isolating, laying out, carving, and burning practice feathers, we can begin to lay out the feathers on the body of the decoy, as shown in Illus. 73.

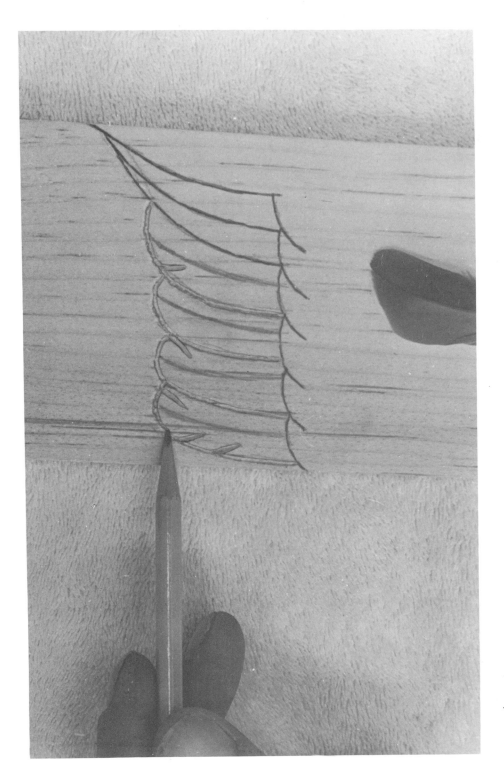

Illus. 67. Doing a practice piece. At right is an actual feather from the secondary group. The group is laid out, carved, and ready to begin burn texturing.

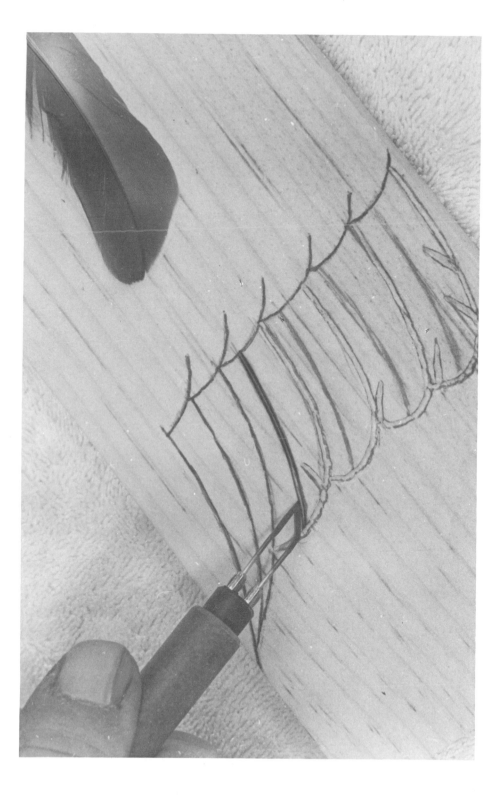

Illus. 68. The first step in burning is to do the shaft with two strokes as shown. Use fairly heavy pressure so these incisions will be sufficiently deeper than the barbs.

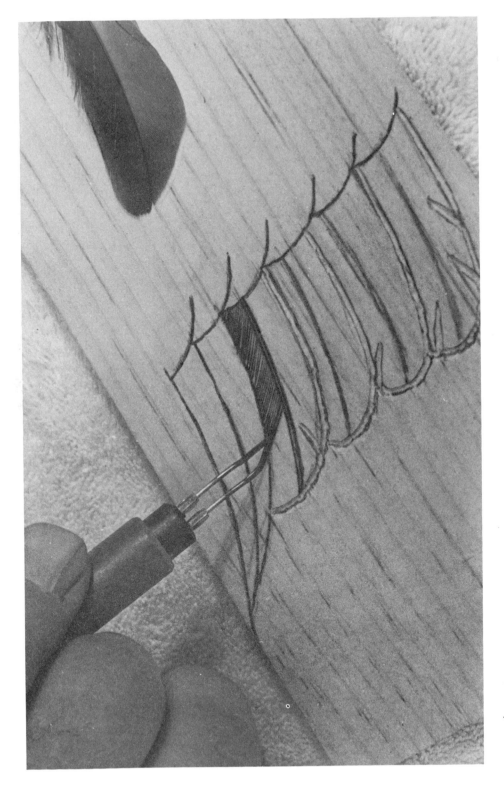

Illus. 69. Burning individual barbs. Work from the shaft toward the outer edge with progressively less pressure toward the outer edges.

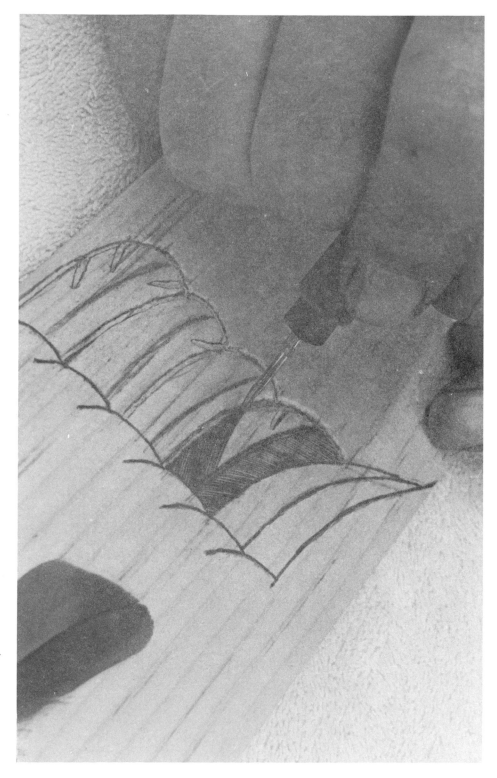

Illus. 70. Repeat the process on the other half of the feather being careful not to burn into the feather-break area. See Illus. 71 showing the unburned break area.

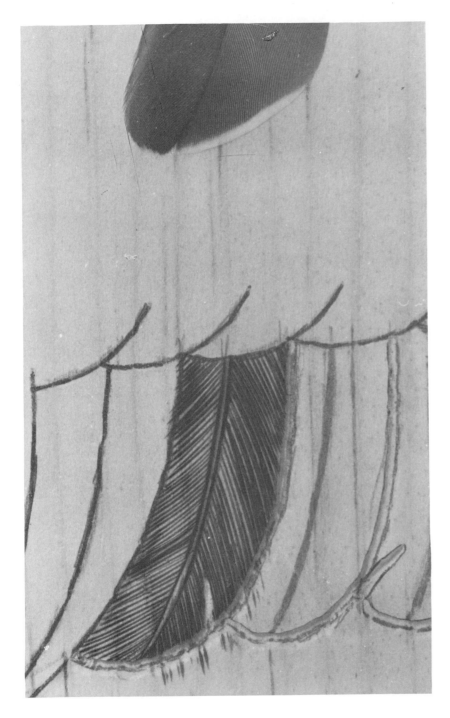

Illus. 71. A completed practice feather—note the unburned area of the "feather break."

Illus. 72. Always remove burned residues from the burned surfaces.

Illus. 73. To start the feathering work on the decoy, draw on the feathers for all of the feather groups.

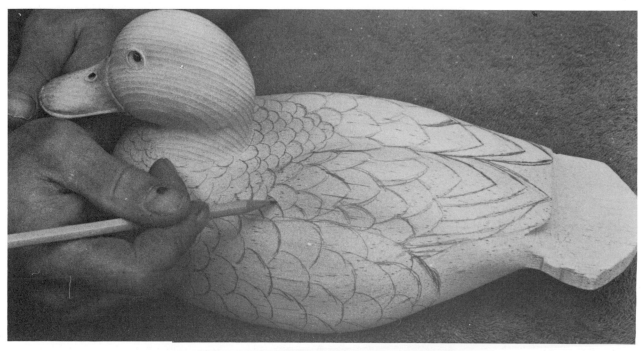

Illus. 74. Since the head is essentially done, begin with the breast area. Do the suggested practice-study piece as shown here, copying an actual feather.

The Breast

Since the head and neck are already done, the next group of feathers to deal with is the breast area (Illus. 74). Be reminded that some species of ducks have tighter breast feathers than others. Consequently, some breast feathers are not just burned, but textured first with a fine-grinding wheel. See Illus. 75. Grinding some of the larger breast feathers first also keeps the carver from developing a set pattern on this area, which can occur when one only burns them. Illus. 76 shows the blending of the breast feathers into the shoulder, cape, and side-pocket area. Notice how the feathers get progressively larger in size as they continue towards the back. Notice also how "feather breaks" begin to occur in the breast area. These are openings on the feather where the hairs have been temporarily matted together. These "breaks" are irregular, and they have no set pattern whatsoever. They can be used by the carver to highlight a certain feather or feather area. Feather breaks can give the carving a sense of action.

Illus. 75. Some species have "tighter" breast feathers than others. In those cases it is best to fine-grind short strokes over the few carved feathers, as shown, that highlight the breast area. This is done prior to burning the individual barbs on all of the feathers in this entire area.

Cape

Illus. 77 shows a study exercise for detailing the cape feathers. These feathers are usually slightly relieved with a small grinding stone as shown in Illus. 78. They may also be ground first with a small wheel

Illus. 76. From the neck, the breast feathers start small and become progressively larger as they proceed down the breast and blend into the shoulder and cape feathers.

before burning. Burning of this group is shown in Illus. 79. It is sometimes helpful to burn the beginning of this feather area by using a rounded burning tip so that you don't dig in at the base of the neck.

Side-Pocket Feathers

An awareness of many little variables or minute, seemingly unimportant details such as depth or texturing, the lapping or shingling pattern of the feathers, and shaft straightness or curvature call attention to the importance of the carver's observation skills. These subtle details can only be put into a carving if the carver is aware of them in the first place.

Illus. 77. Begin a practice-study block of the cape area. (Located behind the neck.)

Illus. 80 shows an actual side-pocket feather and a study exercise of the side-pocket feather group. It is important to note that the size of these feathers are proportionately larger than the breast and cape area

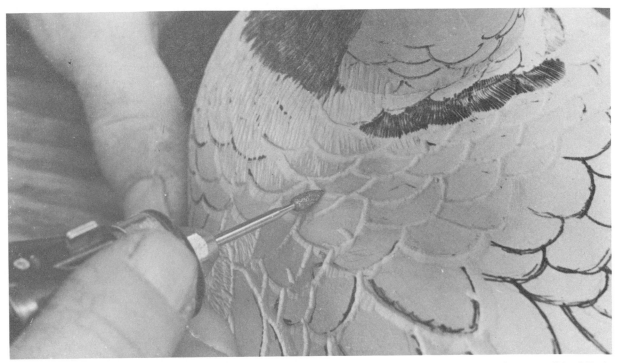

Illus. 78. Cape feathers are first relief carved with a ruby stone bit. Notice that small feather breaks are occasionally visible in this group as they are in all feather groups.

Illus. 79. The relief-carved feathers of the cape area now receive the barb-burning.

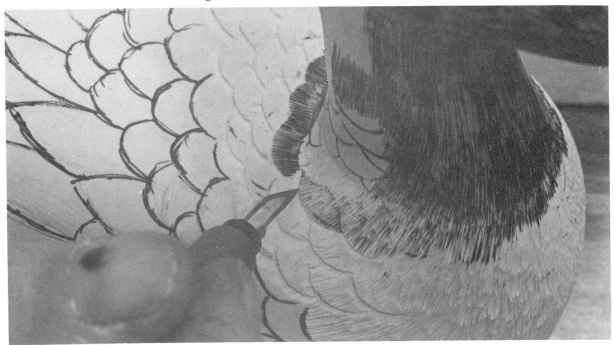

Illus. 80. The side-pocket-feather area is next. Do a practice-study group, copying the real feather as shown here.

feathers. All of the feathers' features now become very visible to the human eye. Each feather is carved in relief with a tapered ruby stone as shown in Illus. 81. Next, grind the surface of each carved feather with a small grinding stone. This tends to blend the feathers together better before they are burned (Illus. 82). Some of these grinding strokes can now become quite deep as there can be quite a bit of feather separation in this area. Also feather breaks can begin to appear proportionally larger.

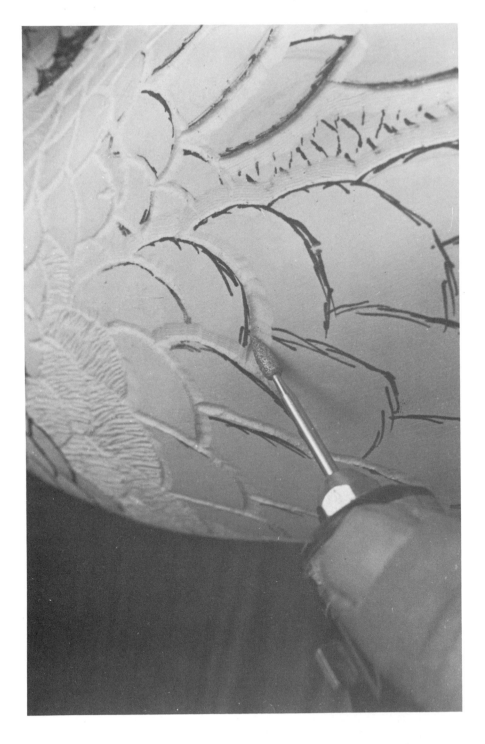

Illus. 81. Using a ruby stone to carve the side-pocket feathers.

Scapular Feathers

These larger feathers extend out of a duck's cape area. Illus. 83 shows the practice study exercise for this group. Illus. 84 shows the group relation to the cape and tertial feather group where they end.

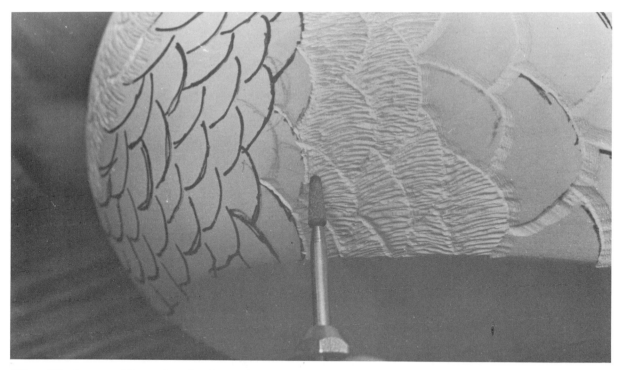

Illus. 82. Larger side-pocket feathers can often be textured with a sharp grinding stone to soften the effect from one feather to another. This is done before burning any of the surface details.

Illus. 83. Next go to the scapular feathers. Do a practice-study piece as shown here, copying a real feather.

Illus. 84. View shows the scapulars. This is the area extending from the cape (above) to the tertials.

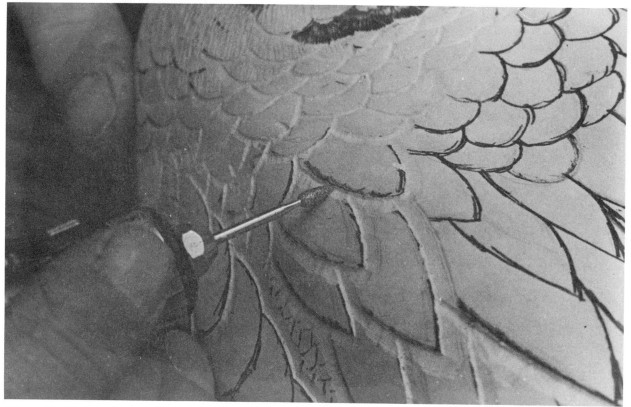

Illus. 85. Relief-carving the scapular feathers with a ruby-stone cutter.

Scapular feathers do change in shape some from one species to another; so it is important to study the duck you are making a carving of. In Illus. 85, we carve the scapular feathers with a ruby stone. Many feather breaks also occur in this area. Most carvers don't grind these feathers before burning them. The feathers of this area have definite barb direction and some feather shafts begin to appear in your carving. Grinding would take away from this. The progression of a typical carving up to this point should look something like the work shown in Illus. 86. Notice how all the feather groups tend to blend together.

Tertials

There are a lot of different styles of tertial feathers from species to species and from male to female. The differences are shown in Illus. 87.

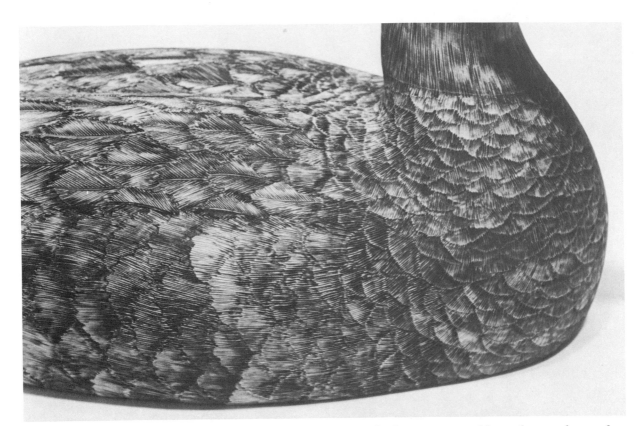

Illus. 86. A look at the neck, breast, cape, side pocket, and scapular feathers all burned and textured. Note how each group blends into the next.

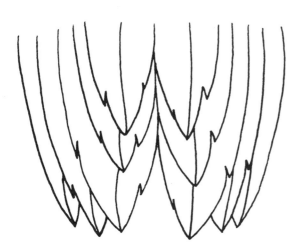

Illus. 87. Drawing of tertial feathers of various species. Left: Mallard and black duck; right: divers. Opposite page: 1. Wood duck drake. 2. Wood duck hen. 3. Shovelers, gadwall, pintail, widgeon, and all teal drakes; 4. Same species as at left, but hens. 5. Hooded merganser drake.

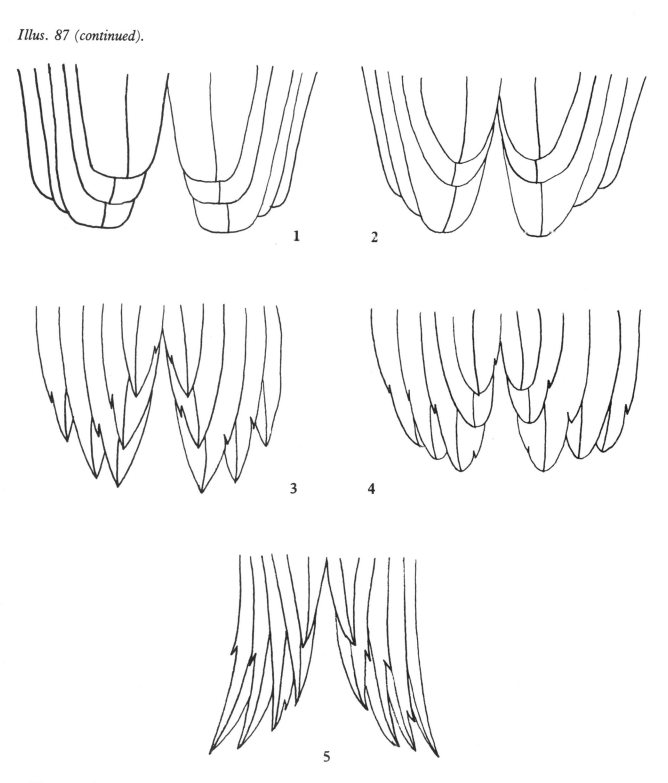

The practice study block (Illus. 88) uses a feather from the same ring-necked duck we have used throughout. Make your own practice piece using feathers for the species you are carving.

Illus. 88. A practice-study piece of a tertial feather group. (This one happens to be of a ring-neck.)

Illus. 89. Since tertials must be more deeply relieved some sanding may be required around each feather.

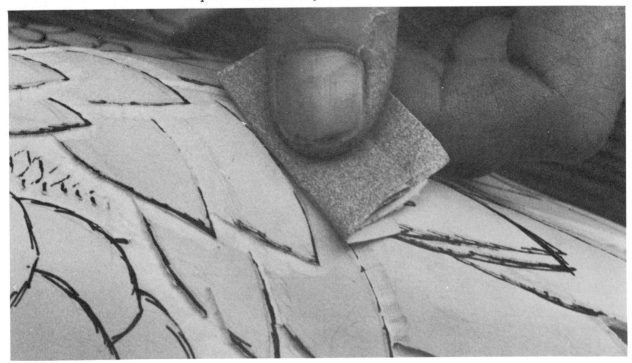

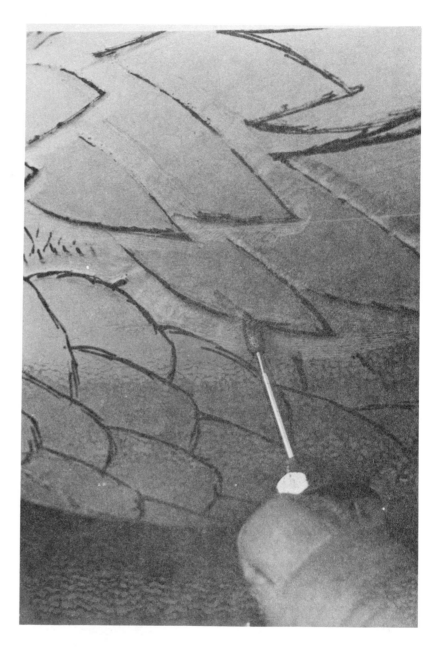

Illus. 90. Carving a ter-tial feather on a pintail drake decoy. Notice the large feather break.

We again relieve the feathers in this area as shown in Illus. 90. Note the large feather break on this tertial feather. Many of these can occur in this area. Some sanding may be required on these feathers because they are relieved quite deeply. (See Illus. 89.) The rear tertials are the largest and are often deeply undercut to give the carving more depth.

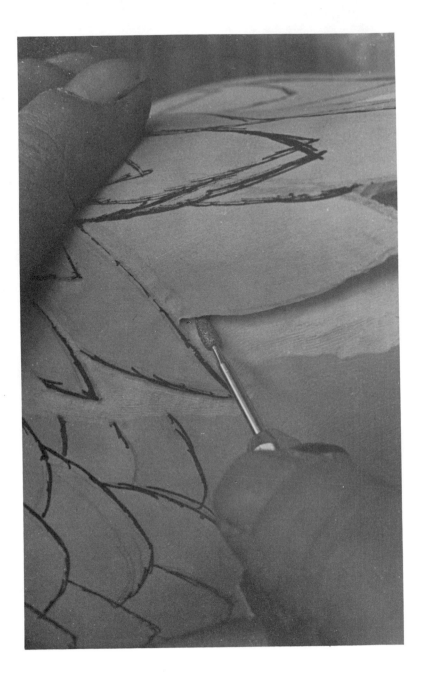

Illus. 91. Undercut the last,
rear tertials.

The underside of the last tertials is also cut away, because this is where the wing raises them off the duck's back as shown in Illus. 91.

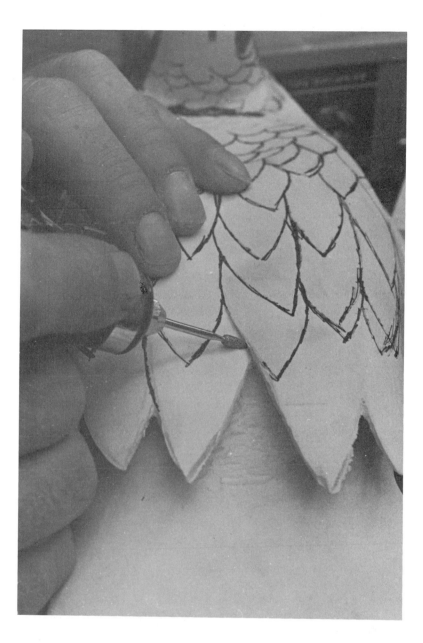

Illus. 92. This illustration shows the right tertial group lapping the left tertial. Also shown here is an undercut being made which will later receive a primary insert.

As we carve the last tertials, we see that one set laps over the other. We must also plan to make our incisions to receive primary inserts if the primaries are to be done separately and inserted. (See Illus. 92.)

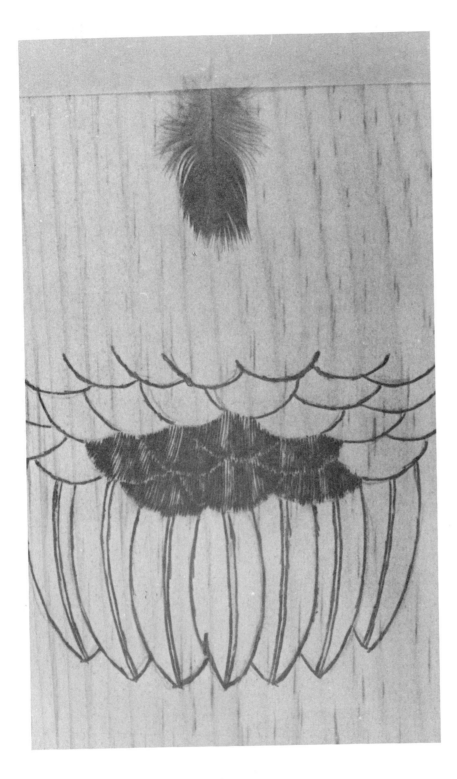

Illus. 93. A practice-study exercise for doing the tail-covert feather group. Notice how similar these are to the breast and cape feathers.

Illus. 94. A view of the lower (underside) tail-covert area. Notice how the underside of the tail feathers are also carved and done in reverse order.

Tail Coverts

Tail coverts are feathers similar to the breast feathers in their size and shape. Tail coverts are located right before a duck's tail feathers on both top and bottom rear. They are also textured in the same manner as the breast feathers. This is illustrated in the study exercise shown in Illus. 93. The detailing of the lower tail coverts is equally important as is seen in Illus. 94.

Tail Feathers

Remember that tail feathers can be either opened or closed. Take this into consideration when you are doing your study exercise as shown in Illus. 95. Tail feathers are individually layered and many feather

Illus. 95. A study-practice piece made for the tail feathers. Note how these are done for the top view shown here as compared to the underside details shown in Illus. 94.

breaks can appear, especially if the tail is fanned. The underside of the tail is carved in reverse order. Refer to Illus. 94. The one that was carved last on the top, now becomes the one carved first on the bottom. At this point we can look closely at the rear half of the carving (Illus. 96) and see how it has all come together. The finished oil-gland coverts are also shown in this photo and they will be dealt with in the next chapter on feather inserts.

Illus. 96. Here are the rear feather groups all carved and burned. Notice the blending together of the various feather groups. This illustration also shows the curled oil-gland coverts (above the tail feathers) unique only to this mallard drake.

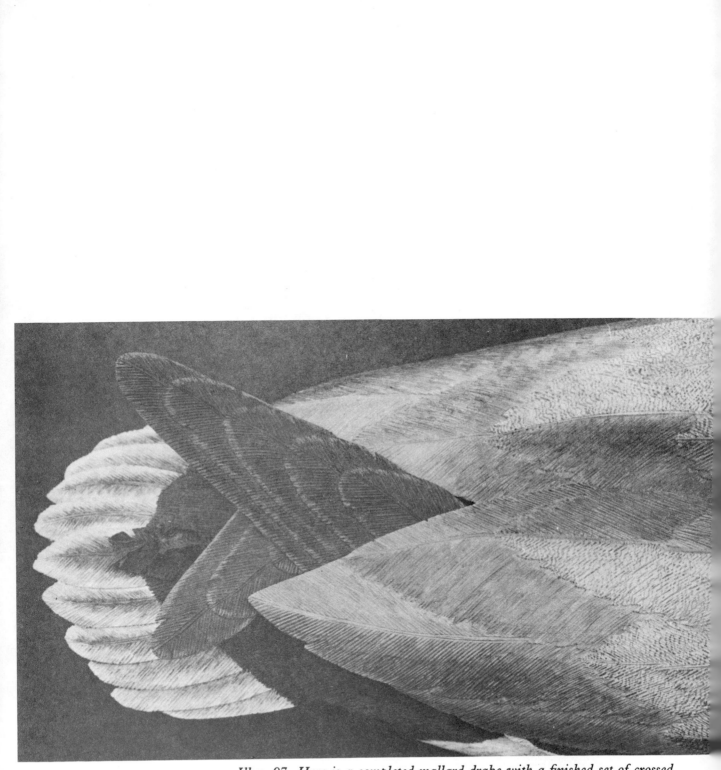

Illus. 97. Here is a completed mallard drake with a finished set of crossed primary inserts.

7. Feather Inserts

Some feathers are more easily carved individually or carved together in small groups and then set into small crevices, which are carved into the duck's body. Feathers of this type are called inserts. This technique is most practical for feathering details in those areas where the feathers extend or project outward, away from the body.

Illus. 98. Some carvings are made with open (uncrossed) primaries as shown here on this red-breasted merganser drake. Open primaries may or may not be carved using inserts.

The use of inserts allows the carver to place feathers in certain positions so they look more realistic (Illus. 97). By using separate pieces of wood the insert areas are also made to be much stronger. The use of an insert permits the carver to utilize the optimum strength of the wood by orienting the grain direction so that it runs with the length of the feather(s) no matter how it's placed on the duck. Consequently, this technique not only simplifies the carving process, it makes the carving of realistic feathers easier and stronger. The projected feathers are not weakened by cross-grain structure which would result if carved in any other way.

Primaries. Inserts are commonly used for making the primary feathers. The primaries, as we know, are carved either in a crossed position, as shown in Illus. 97, or they are made open, as shown on the decoy in Illus. 98. Inserts can be used to effect either of these two basic positions of the primaries. However, inserts are almost always used on realistic decoys when their primaries are in the crossed position, as in Illus. 97. Illus. 99 shows some actual primary feathers taken from a real ring-necked duck. Make a layout and burn the feathers on a practice block as we did in chapters 5 and 6. (See Illus. 100.)

Illus. 99. Actual primary feathers from a real ring-necked duck.

94

The material used for making feather inserts can be of several choices. Some carvers use thin strips cut from the same wood block used for the body. Others use a thin cut of a flexible hardwood such as holly. Basswood strips are widely used because of their availability in hobby and craft shops. Tongue depressors will do the job too. Today, a special, very thin plywood called "Sig" plywood is also available for making inserts. Making inserts with this material is discussed below.

Illus. 100. Practice-study work piece of relief carved and burned texturing primary feathers.

Illus. 101. Right and left primary feather groups laid out and cut to the profile shape.

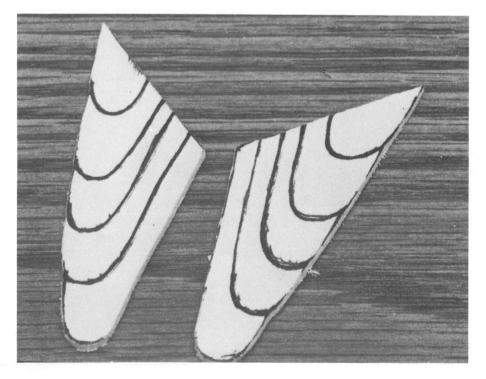

Illus. 102. Checking the primaries for preliminary fit into the tertial areas.

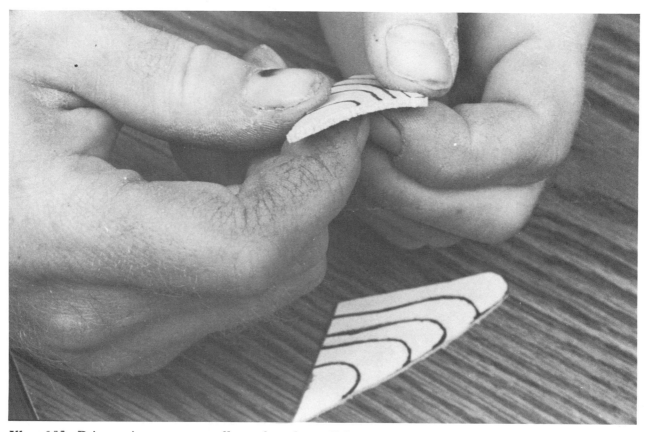

Illus. 103. Primary inserts are usually made to have slight cross-sectional curves.

The first method and example for making the primary inserts will utilize basswood slices about ⅛ inch thick. Illus. 101 shows them laid out and cut to profile shape. Next, check for the approximate fit into the tertial area where they will be inserted. (See Illus. 102.) The inserts should be curved slightly cross-sectionally as shown in Illus. 103. This can be accomplished by soaking the insert in water to make it pliable. Then bend it over a large dowel, using a rubber band to hold it in the curved position until dry.

Once satisfied with the shape and fit of the insert, carve the individual feather layers as shown in Illus. 104. Some feather breaks are usually evident and should not be overlooked while carving these feather inserts. Illus. 105 shows a finished set of primary inserts ready to be glued into place. However, before gluing the inserts into the body crevices, which incidentally are cut by power carving or with a

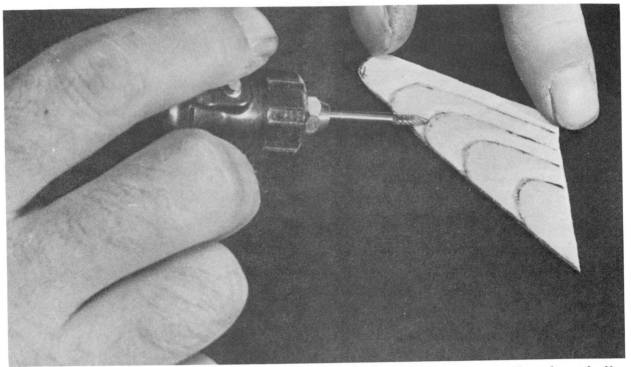

Illus. 104. Relieving each individual feather provides a layered effect.

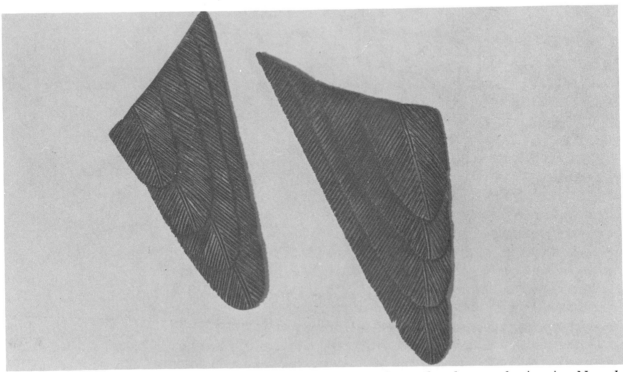

Illus. 105. The finished set of carved and textured primaries. Note the "layering" of each insert.

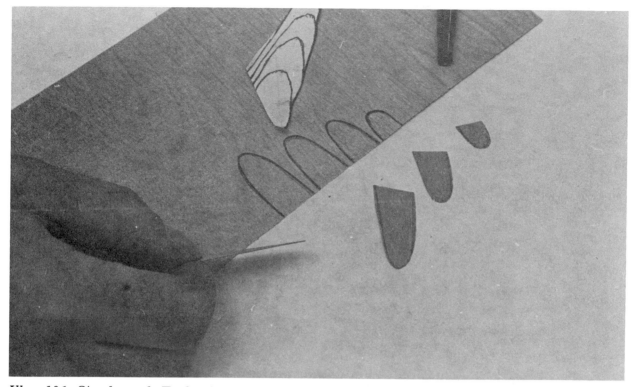

Illus. 106. Sig plywood. Each primary feather is laid out individually. Note how thin this feather material is.

very hot burning tool, consider prepainting. It might be a whole lot easier to completely paint the inserts, especially the undersides, and the surrounding areas as these surfaces may be very difficult to reach later. This is especially true when doing the crossed type of primaries. Refer to chapter 8 for more details about painting and installing the primary inserts.

"Sig" Plywood Inserts. "Sig" plywood is an extremely thin, very strong three-ply plywood. It's paper-like in thickness and very flexible. (See Illus. 106.) Sig plywood has been used for some time in model-making, and it has begun to be regarded as a good material for feather inserts on decoys. Since it doesn't split easily, and it is thin and flexible, it is cut easily with household scissors (Illus. 107). Inserts made of sig plywood are such that each individual cutout is the thickness of one simulated feather. After each feather of the primary group, for example, has been cut out, they are individually burned, layer-stacked, and glued together to make a primary feather insert unit. (See Illus. 108 to 110.)

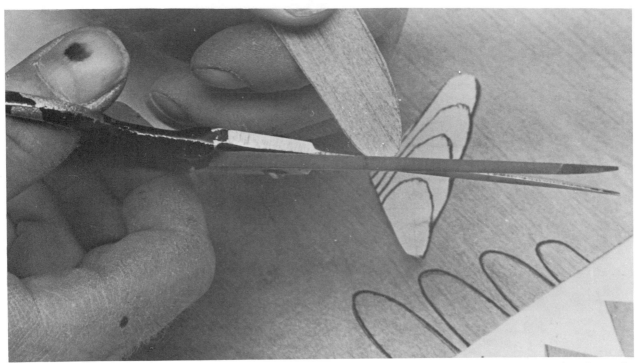

Illus. 107. Use a scissors to cut sig plywood.

Illus. 108. Burning the underside of the largest primary feather in its group.

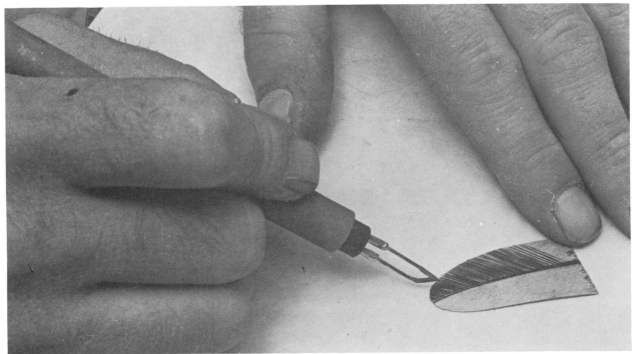

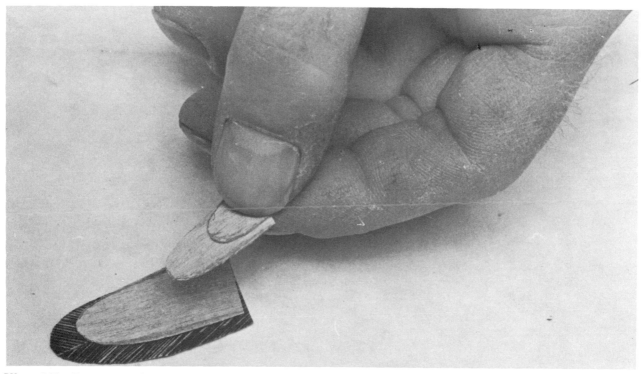

Illus. 109. Demonstrating the stacking or layering technique of insert-making.

Illus. 110. Checking the flexibility of this plywood material.

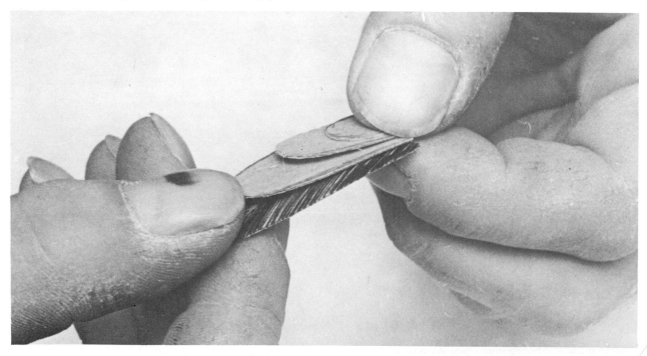

Illus. 111. A view showing the completed oil-gland coverts on the mallard drake.

Illus. 112. A closeup look at an actual oil-gland covert feather at left. The formed, simulated feather at right, an initial layout on sheet lead is shown in the foreground.

When burning these sig plywood feathers, it is essential to burn the underside first. This will cause and give each feather the cross-sectional curve desired. The major advantage of sig plywood inserts is the extreme flexibility of this material. On a finished decoy, the protruding primaries are generally very fragile and thus easily broken. Using sig plywood and inserted primaries greatly reduces these possibilities.

Oil-Gland Coverts. This curled set of feathers is peculiar only to the mallard drake (Illus. 111). One real covert, taken from an actual duck, is shown in Illus. 112. The easiest way to simulate the curl of such feathers in your carving is not to make them out of wood, but to make them out of thin sheet lead (Illus. 112). The best and most economical source for this lead material is found on the inside of an old car battery.

Illus. 113 through 117 show the steps involved to make a single oil-gland covert. Remember that the mallard requires two feathers. Be especially careful when cutting in the feather breaks. It is best to make slight cuts at the start and bend. Make deeper cuts as needed. Bend the lead slowly and carefully. Lead is very soft and will tear if not done properly.

Illus. 113. The sheet lead is cut easily with a household scissors.

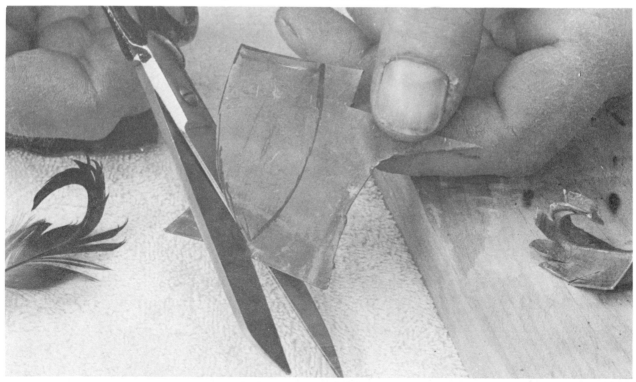

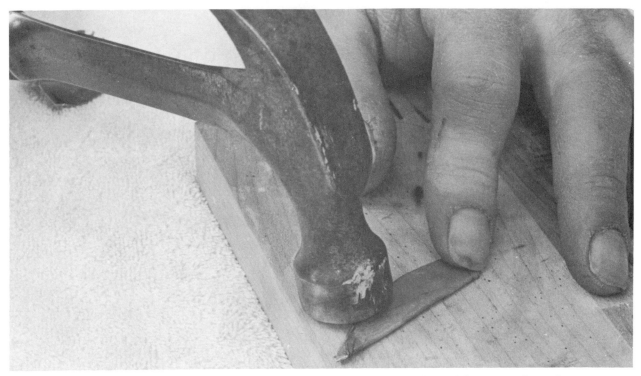

Illus. 114. Fold and hammer along the vane area.

Illus. 115. Cutting out the feather breaks also makes the lead more bendable.

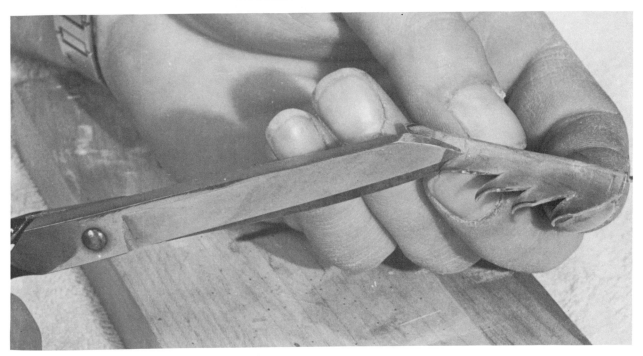

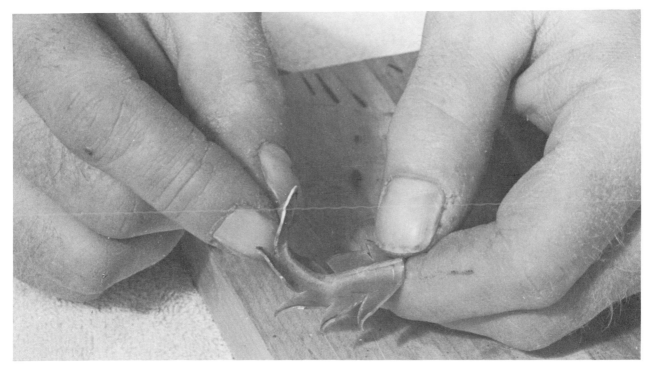

Illus. 116. Test bend.

Illus. 117. Texture the surface with a rotary tool before bending to its final curved shape. Note the formed shape of the feather shaft resulting from the hammering step.

Illus. 118. A finished set of oil-gland coverts inserted on the duck. Note how they visually blend with the surrounding textured area.

Now carve small recesses or slits into the upper-tail coverts to receive the oil-gland covert inserts. Glue them into place with one of the so-called "super" glues and add necessary filler to the surrounding area. Texture and burn the filled area so that it blends with the other feathers in the area. The finished product is shown in Illus. 118.

Tail Feather Inserts. This type of insert is used in making the long curved tail feathers typical of either the pintail drake or the old squaw drake. A harder species of wood may be selected for added strength.

First make a pattern of the necessary feathers and saw out the shape with a band saw. Soak the cut-out piece in water until soft. Bend it in the simple jig shown in Illus. 119 until dry. Check the location of the insert (Illus. 120), and outline the area to be recessed.

Illus. 119. Bending a long tail insert.

Illus. 120. Checking the location for a tail-feather insert.

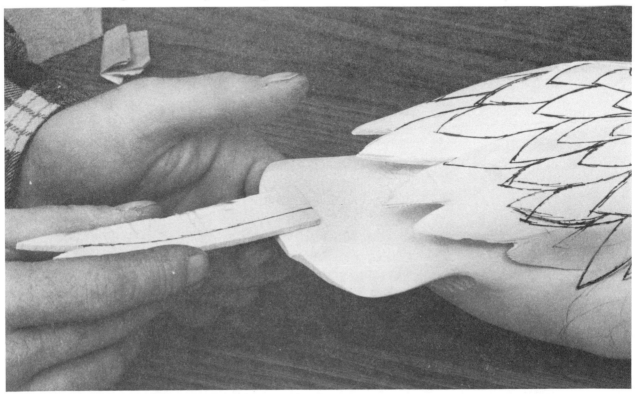

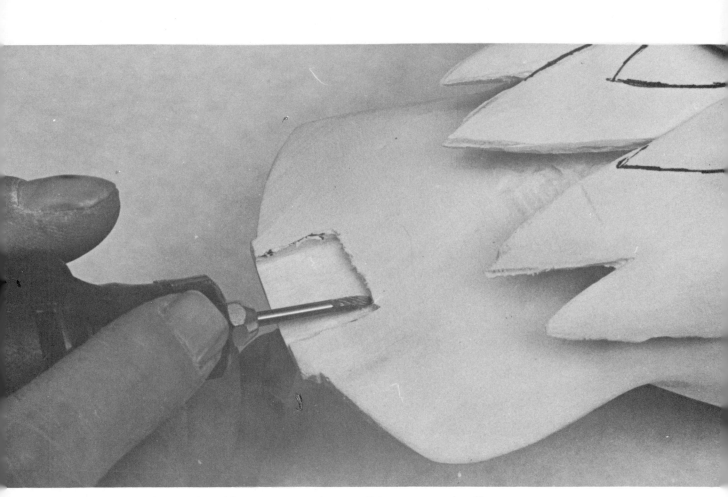

Illus. 121. Grinding makes this recess to receive a tail insert on a pintail.

A recess is carved into the upper-tail covert area (Illus. 121). The insert is glued and clamped into place as shown in Illus. 122. Fill any cracks with filler. Now carve the entire area of the upper-tail coverts and the tail feathers.

The preceding describes and illustrates the basic techniques for using inserts to your advantage. Other carvers use inserts in a wide variety of different ways. Entire wings can be carved and inserted. Inserts have even been made for crest areas, and some carvers insert tertial feathers and each individual feather of the tail section. Although the essential purpose for using inserts is to gain added strength, some very artistic effects can be achieved with inserts. Let your creative ability be your guide. Overdoing it can create problems. Inserts must look natural, fit tightly, and be fastened securely.

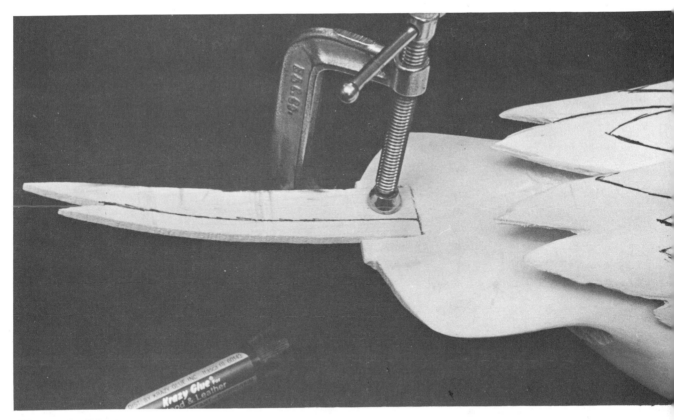

Illus. 122. The insert glued into place.

Illus. 123. The first step is to prepare the surface with the application of a finish-sealer applied over the entire surface.

8. Painting

This chapter covers the fundamental technical considerations and preliminary steps needed to paint a realistic decoy. It also presents a fairly involved step-by-step demonstration of the painting and finishing off of one realistic decoy example. The scope and depth of painting instructions necessary to cover all of the procedures involved to paint every species of duck cannot possibly be included here. Nor have we included specific formulas for mixing the various complex shades or color tones necessary to imitate nature's special color spectrums that are characteristic to the thirty or so most popular species. This subject alone could fill volumes and, perhaps, if so done, it would contain much useless wordy information because, in the end, the final color is achieved by trial-and-error mixing. The final color is also a matter of personal choice, personal interpretation, and definitely a matter of individual artistic expression.

Illus. 124. Acrylic paints dry fast, blend well, and reduce or clean up conveniently with water.

The step-by-step illustrated demonstration covers a typical set of procedures. It is intended only as a suggestive guideline and to show one way of painting a realistic decoy. The decoy selected for this demonstration is a bluebill drake with crossed primary inserts. It has most of the essential features requiring expressive painting skills common to most other duck species. Therefore, the techniques shown in this chapter can pretty well be applied to realistic painting of other ducks. Only the colors will be different.

Do as we have done in learning to lay out, carve, and texture the various feather groups. Take the study practice blocks imitating real feathers, and practice painting them before going on to your carved decoy. Be sure to use good visual aids and color references in selecting and matching colors. Refer also to our color section following page 64.

Sealing the Surface (Illus. 123). Sealing the carving is a very important step, especially if one is to enter competitions where ducks are judged while floating in water. Most of today's carvers use lacquer-based sealers that are thinned down to a 50:50 ratio with lacquer thinner. This mixture penetrates the wood and it doesn't fill up the fine burning lines, obliterating the texture as a varnish would. Lacquers also dry rapidly, which means you can get to the actual painting sooner. *Lacquer-based mixtures are highly flammable, so caution should be used.*

Paints. The two main types of paints used are either oil or acrylics. (See Illus. 124.) Each has its own distinct set of advantages and disadvantages.

Oil paints are very easily blended and dry very slowly. This gives the carver more time to mix his colors and get them right. Also, if he isn't satisfied with the look he has achieved, while they are still wet, oils can be wiped off and the carver can start all over again.

Acrylics are water-based plastic paints that dry quite rapidly and are easily reduced with water (Illus. 125). These paints do blend well, but this work has to be done quite rapidly because of the quick-drying qualities. Some carvers like to hold their decoy in their hands as they paint and this can be done more easily when acrylics are used. Acrylics also allow you to clean your brushes in water. Many artists use a drying medium with acrylics. This retards the drying process and allows more time for mixing and blending.

Though more and more carvers seem to be leaning towards the use

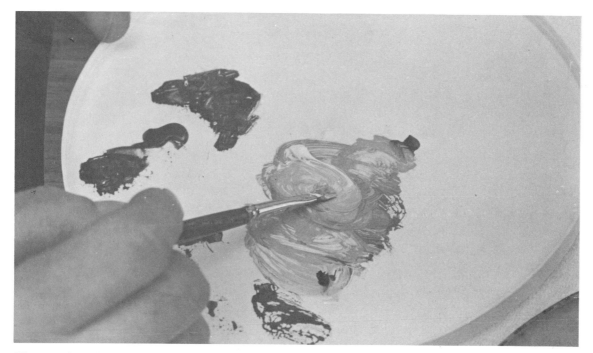

Illus. 125. Mixing acrylic paints on a plastic cover.

of acrylic paint, don't totally rule out the use of oils until you have tried them. What is best and what is the most comfortable for you is of the utmost importance in the choice of paints.

Brushes (Illus. 126). The number of different kinds of brushes available to the artist is almost unbelievable. However, some carvers buy specific brushes and, with a scissors, fashion them to their specific needs for painting certain parts of the anatomy. Determine which ones best fit your needs. If any word of advice can be given here, it is to start with a smaller brush and progressively use larger ones. As your blending techniques advance, you will discover exactly what brush you need to do the job. You will also find out that some of the intricate details can only be done with the smallest brush available and that there is just no other way, even though using a small brush often takes more time.

The only definite guideline in brush selection is to be sure to use a type of brush compatible with the type of paint you are using. Only use synthetic-hair brushes with synthetic paints and natural-hair brushes with oil-based paints. Your brushes will last much longer and stay in much better shape. Remember to thoroughly clean brushes for longer brush life.

Illus. 126. A basic selection of artist's brushes.

Bronzing Powders and Iridescent Paints. Capturing nature's vast array of iridescent colors is one of the most complex problems facing the carver. These colors are impossible to duplicate but can be imitated with some degree of success. A considerable amount of experimentation is necessary. Some artists prefer to mix the metallic powders into their blended paint colors. Others prefer to mix metallic paint with their blended color. Still others prefer to thin the paint or powder and apply it as a thin metallic film over their previously applied blended color. Realism is the key word here. Too much metallic can look gaudy and unnatural. Too little won't show up at all. One must practice this process many times to achieve some success.

Some Painting Tips. The burned surface of a decoy (before it has been painted) usually has a deep natural umber color. This is a very natural color in nature and can be used to advantage to enhance your carving. This is especially true on areas of the carving that are black or white. Some surfaces that appear as black and white are not really. Upon a close examination of a real bird you'll find that both of these colors actually have a slight amount of umber tone in them. If one is careful, and applies the first coats in a very thin wash, the umber tone of the burning will show through these base colors. Remember, a "wash" is an application or a coat of well-thinned paint. Putting on successive coats in thin washes allows better control of how much color is being added. This also leaves less chance of filling in the fine burned texture with too much paint. Two things must be mentioned here. It will take more coats of the white over the burned surface to achieve the color you want than it will of the black. Dark colors eat up light ones and the white color you put over a dark surface today may look two shades darker tomorrow when it has dried thoroughly. The reverse is true for the black. Seeing that the umber color of the burning is lighter than the black, it will cover faster and disappear with less coats over it. As you progress, you will develop many painting tricks of your own. The various methods and techniques are many and varied. Practice is essential and patience is of the utmost importance.

Vermiculations. Close examination of the many and various duck feathers often show a series of broken lines and dots on them. When all these feathers are grouped together in a set the entire area appears to look like a series of wavy lines. Some of these lines are quite broad and intense as on the side-pocket area of the drake wood duck. Others are very fine and subtle, like those on the mallard drake. In either case, making these look real is another difficult task faced by the carver.

For many years, the most common practice was to use a pen and india ink applied as a series of broken lines of the necessary thickness. The greatest drawback to this method came from trying to make these lines look more subtle after they were applied. No ink is truly permanent and when thin-wash coats were applied over these lines, the ink would tend to run and give the entire surface a chalky look.

In recent years, many carvers have begun using acrylic paint, thinned to a watery consistency. It is applied with a pen in the same, traditional manner. When dry, the lines are truly permanent and can be washed over with no fear of them running. Another advantage is color. Not all vermiculations are black. Some are grey, some are brown, and some are even white. The variety of vermiculation colors is endless and can be duplicated successfully when using acrylics. You can blend any color you wish. Remember, it is harder to achieve a true color when applying a thinned light color over a dark one than it is to obtain a desired dark color when applied over a light one. Keep these painting tips in mind as you observe the step-by-step painting of the bluebill shown in the remaining photos. Study Illus. 127 through 167.

Illus. 127. Starting to paint the bluebill begins with painting the tail coverts and the underside of the tertails. Use a mixture of black and a small amount of burnt umber.

Illus. 128. Paint the tertial area with a mixture of burnt umber with small amounts of black and white.

Illus. 129. The rear body area has been painted. Paint the primary inserts with burnt umber. Lighten the edges with a mixture of burnt umber and white.

Illus. 130. Using one of the "super" glues or a quick-set epoxy, glue in the first insert, which is the lower primaries.

Illus. 131. Use folded paper or anything to support the primary until the glue sets.

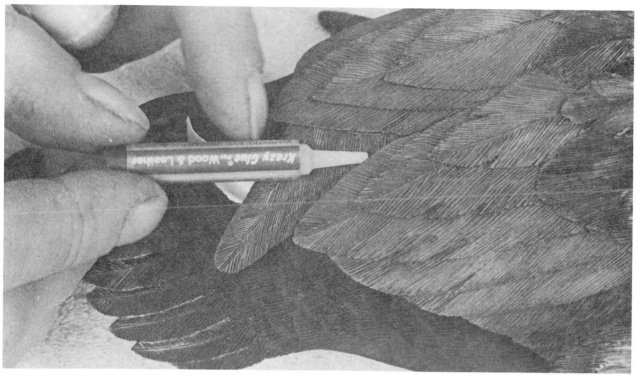

Illus. 132. Glue applied to the groove that will receive the upper primary insert.

Illus. 133. Both primaries now set in place.

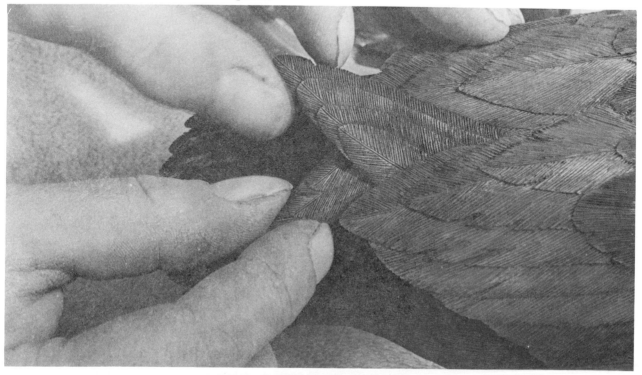

Illus. 134. Paint the wing coverts, which are located above the secondary feathers, black.

Illus. 135. Paint the speculum area (secondary feathers) white.

Illus. 136. Paint the outer section of the secondary feathers black.

Illus. 137. Highlight the black area of the secondaries so the outer edges result in a lighter color.

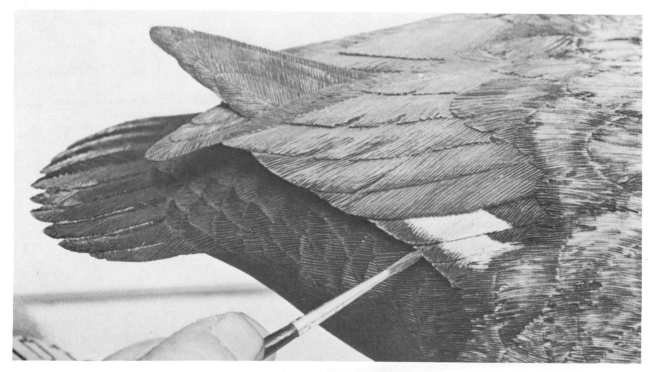

Illus. 138. Paint the tail feathers, using burnt umber mixed with a small amount of white.

Illus. 139. Paint the underside of the tail feathers in the same manner.

Illus. 140. Highlight all edges of the tail feathers with a mixture of white and a small amount of burnt umber.

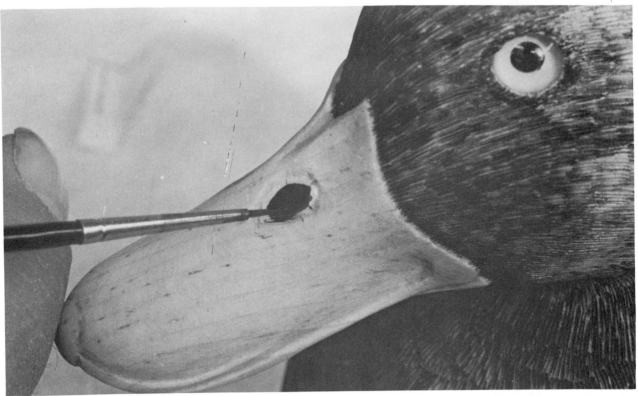

Illus. 141. At any time paint the inside of the nostril black.

Illus. 142. Wash the breast area with several coats of black with a small amount of burnt umber.

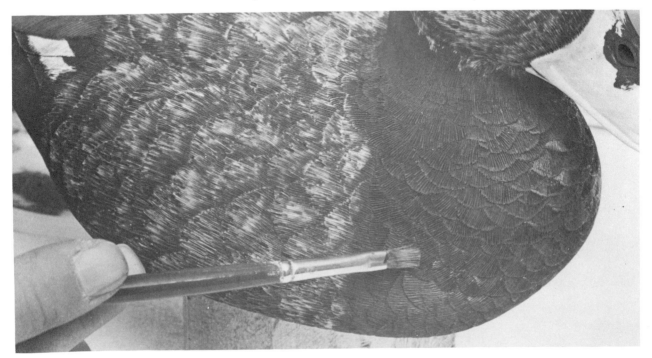

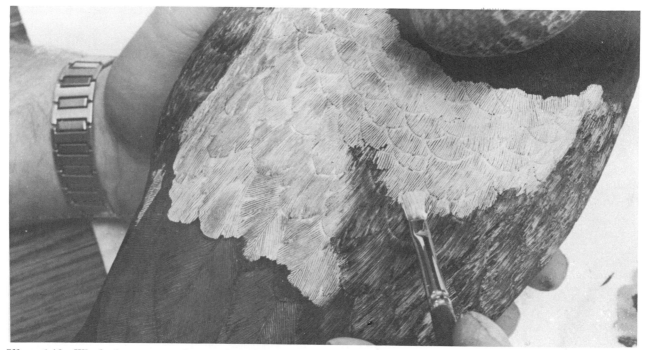

Illus. 143. Wash the cape and scapulars with several coats of white base.

Illus. 144. Since the tertials and secondary areas are all finish-painted, be careful when applying the whitewash coats. Brush away from the finished areas.

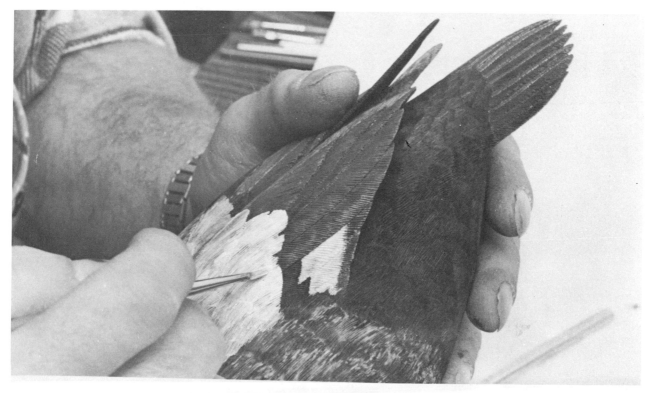

Illus. 145. Several coats of whitewash are also applied to the side-pocket area.

Illus. 146. Now the head. Apply base wash coats of green mixed with a small quanity of black.

Illus. 147. To highlight the cheek area, add a small amount of cadmium yellow. Blend this into the previously applied green and black mixture while it is still wet.

Illus. 148. Paint the underside of the bill using a mixture of ultramarine blue, black and white.

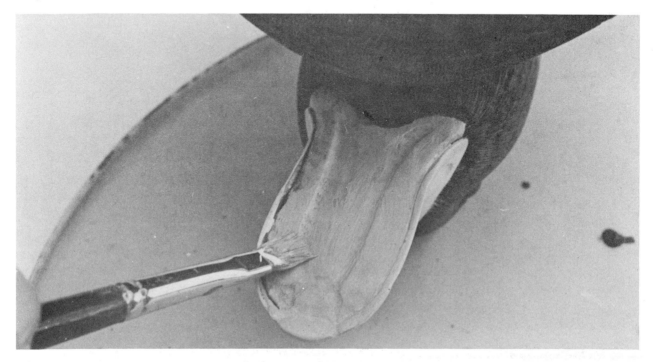

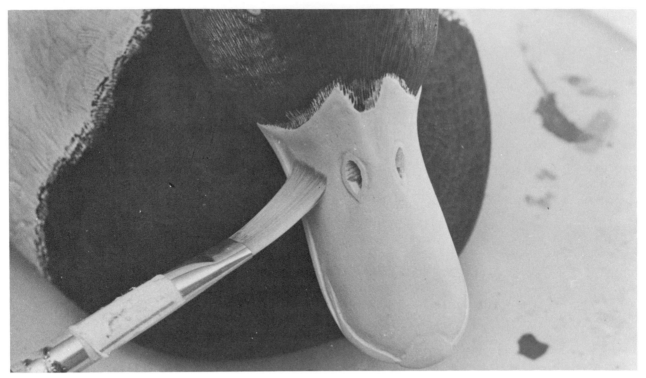

Illus. 149. Paint the upper bill using a mixture of white with a small amount of ultramarine blue.

Illus. 150. Paint the upper nail black.

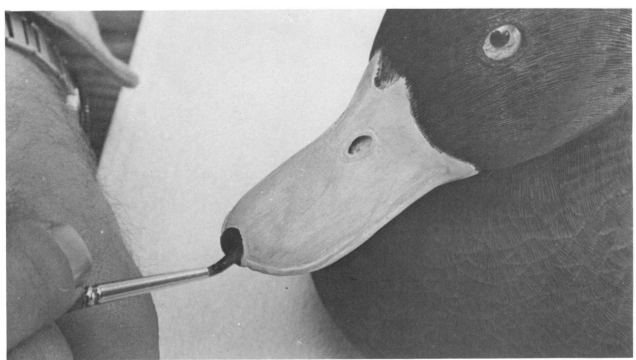

128

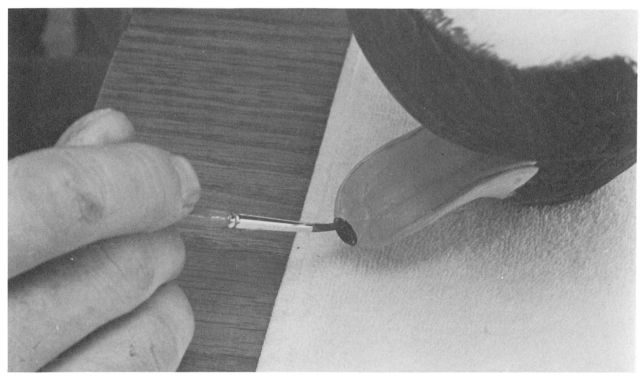

Illus. 151. And paint the lower nail black.

Illus. 152. Touch up the inside of the nostril with black.

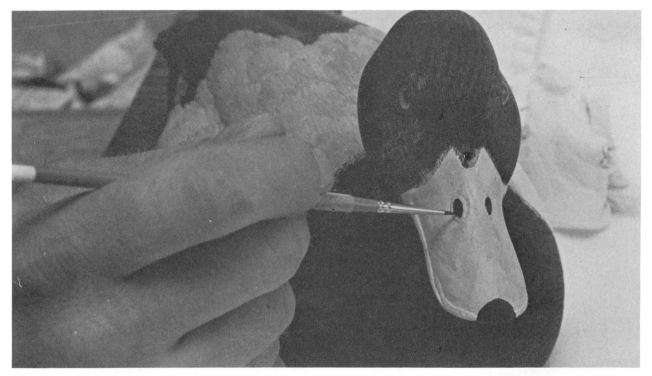

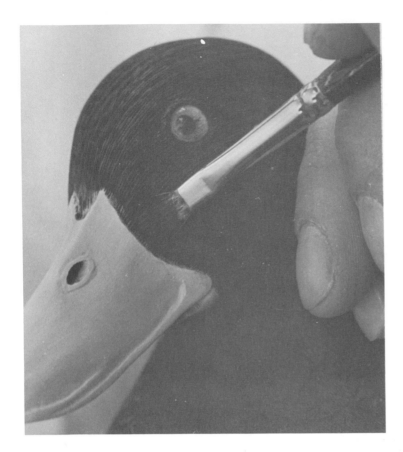

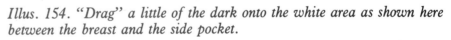

Illus. 153. Using the green mixtures, go back and touch up the area where the bill and head join.

Illus. 154. "Drag" a little of the dark onto the white area as shown here between the breast and the side pocket.

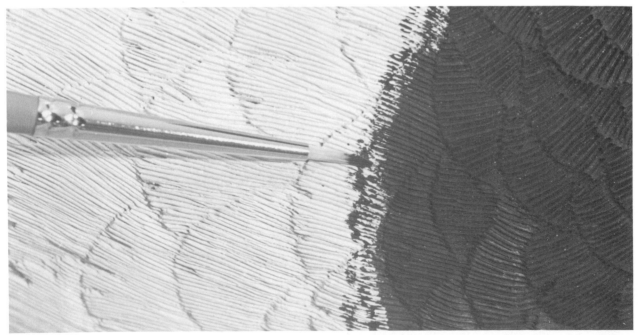

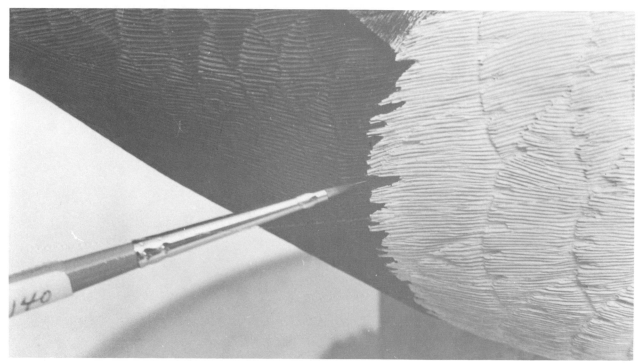

Illus. 155. Using the dark color, touch up the area between the rear side pocket and the lower tail coverts.

Illus. 156. The scapular area can now be washed with a mixture of white and a small amount of burnt umber. Apply so the tone gets darker as it progresses to the rear.

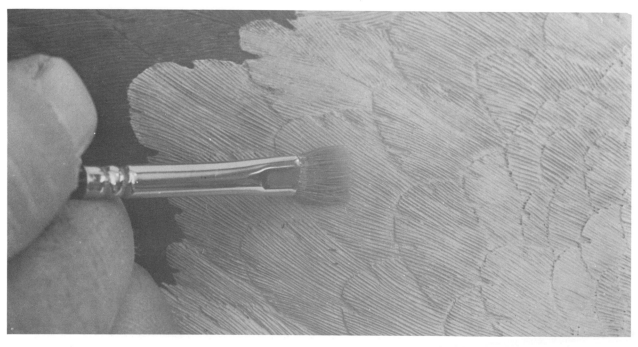

Illus. 157. Vermiculations are now added, using thinned black acrylic paint.

Illus. 158. Vermiculating the entire side-pocket, cape, and scapular areas.

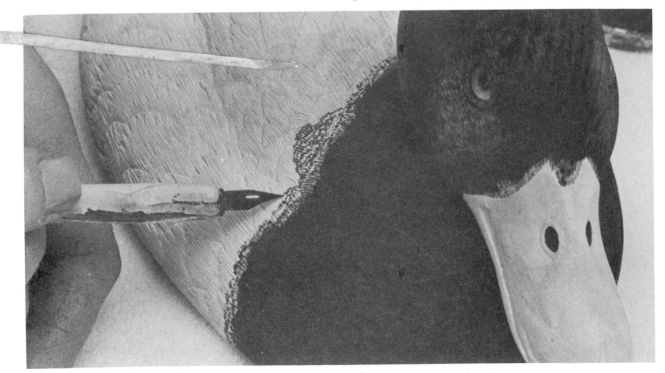

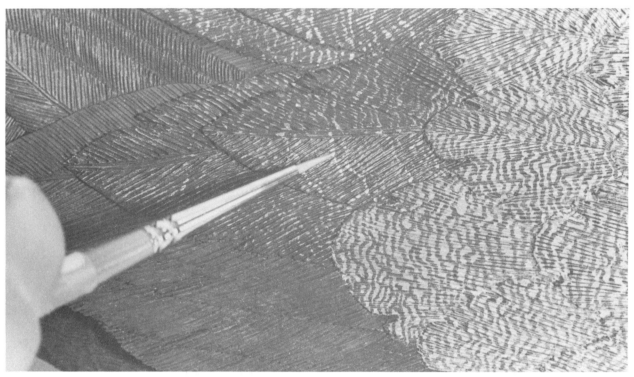

Illus. 159. Vermiculating the darker tertial feathers, using a thinned white acrylic applied with a fine brush as shown.

Illus. 160. With thinned white acrylic, wash the entire pocket area to make the vermiculations more subtle.

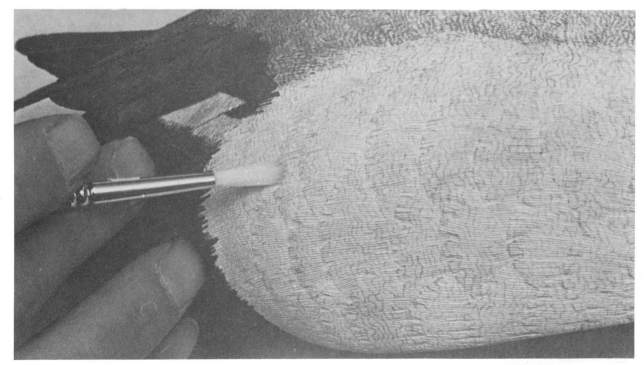

Illus. 161. Washing is likewise done to the scapular area.

Illus. 162. A small amount of burnt umber is added to the whitewash to darken the rear scapular feathers.

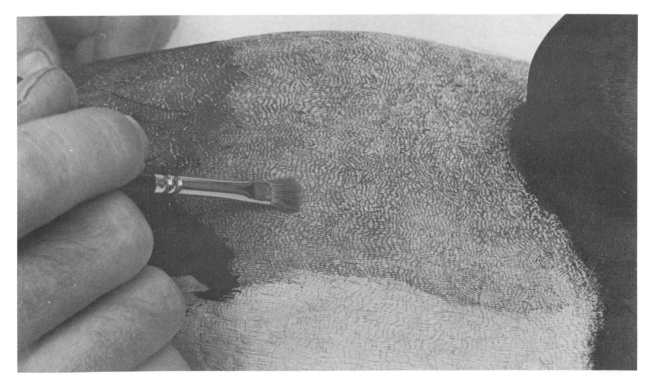

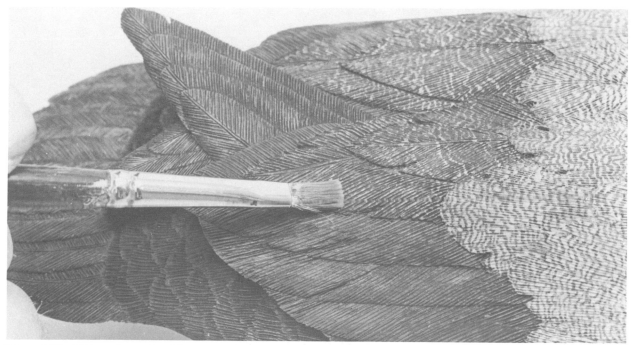

Illus. 163. Thinned wash of burnt umber is applied to the white vermiculations on the tertial area. This makes them look less pronounced.

Illus. 164. Doing the coverts. Use a dry brush with just a "dab" of unthinned burnt umber. Drag the brush over the surface with a very slight stippling action so the paint only highlights the covert area. The paint should only take on the higher surfaces of the textured feather.

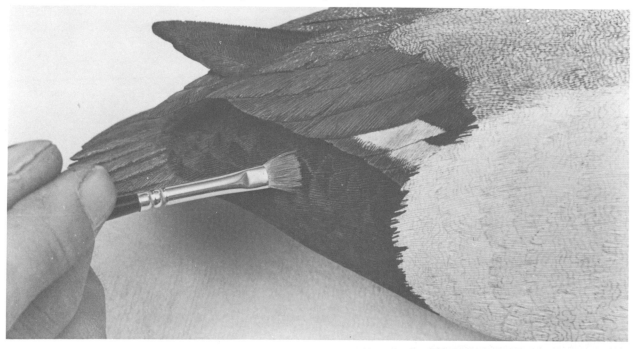

Illus. 165. "Touch" the outer edges of the tail feathers with a lighter shade of burnt umber.

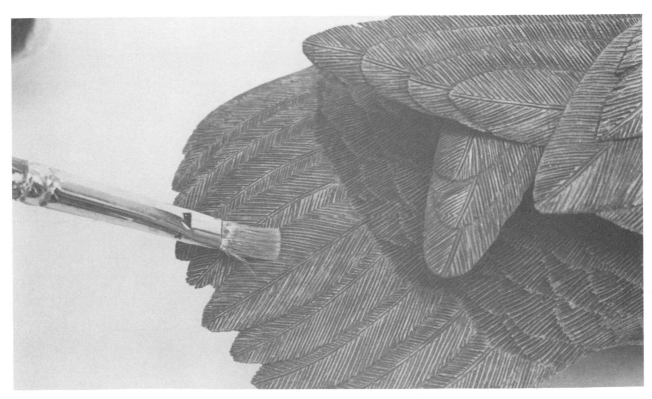

Illus. 166. Using the "dry brush technique" with a lightened shade of the same burnt umber used previously, highlight all of the tail feathers.

Illus. 167. Signing and dating your work is a must.

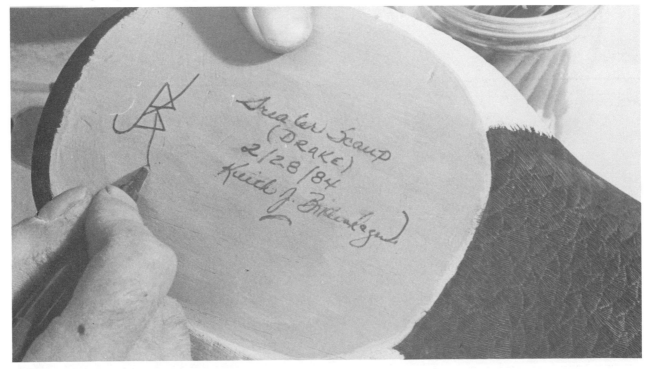

Illus. 168. Head details.

9. Looking at a Bluebill

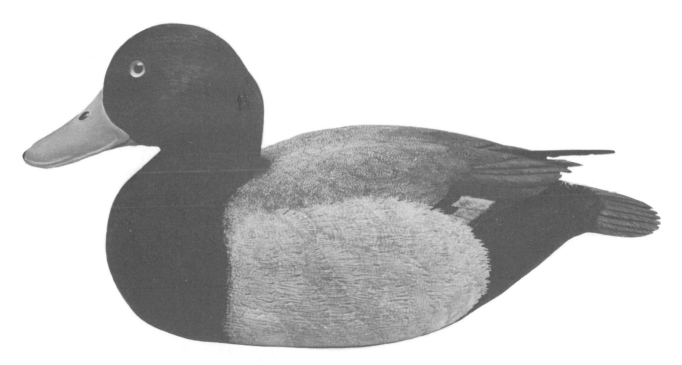

Illus. 169. The greater scaup drake (bluebill).

Illus. 170. Close-up of bill.

Illus. 171. Eye and eyelid.

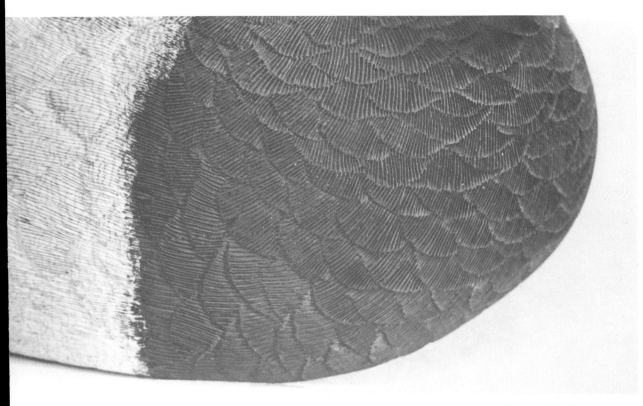

Illus. 172. Breast area and where it joins the side pocket.

Illus. 173. Close-up of the side feathers. Note the subtle vermiculations.

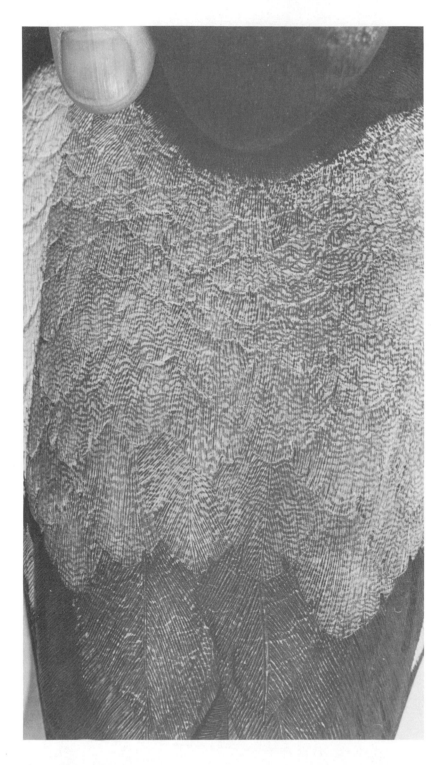

Illus. 174. Top view showing the vermiculated cape, scapular and tertial feathers.

Illus. 175. View of tertial and primary feather groups.

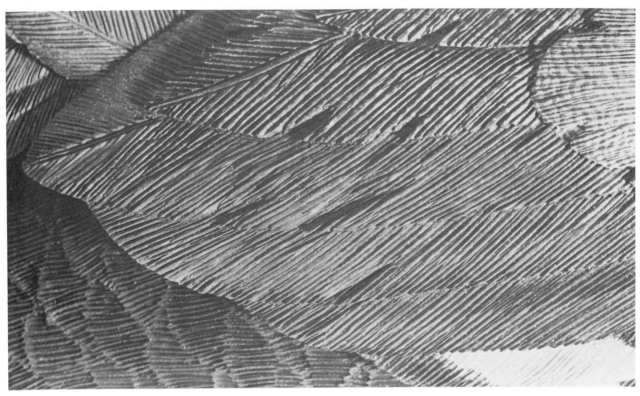

Illus. 176. Close-up of right tertial feather group.

Illus. 177. The right primary insert and how it meets the right tertials.

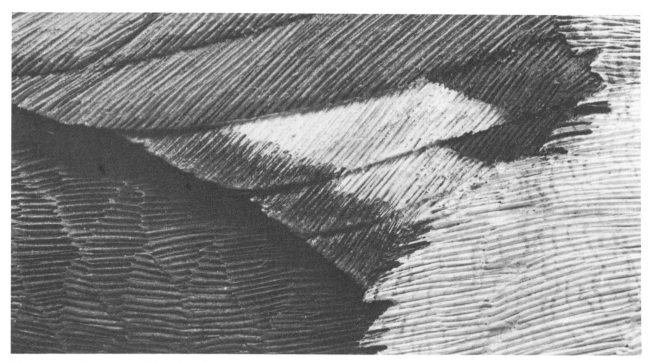

Illus. 178. Close-up of the right secondary feathers.

Illus. 179. Top view of the bluebill's tail.

Illus. 180. Head profile.

10. Looking at the Canvasback Drake

Illus. 181. The canvasback drake (from the collection of Tom "Shipwreck" Kelly).

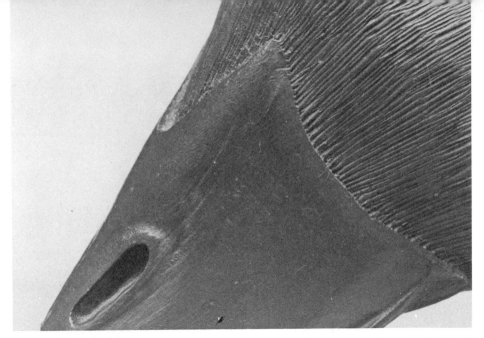

Illus. 182. The bill meets the head.

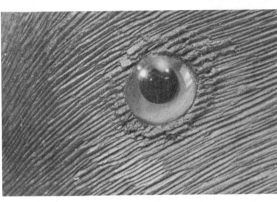

Illus. 183. Eye and lid close-up.

Illus. 184. Overall top view of the canvasback's body.

Illus. 185. View of breast, shoulder, and the beginning of the side-pocket area.

Illus. 186. Top view showing the cape, scapular, and tertial areas.

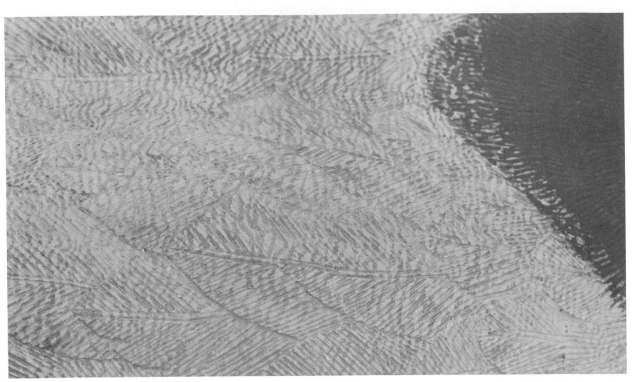

Illus. 187. Close-up where the cape section joins the scapulars.

Illus. 188. Close-up of secondaries and wing coverts.

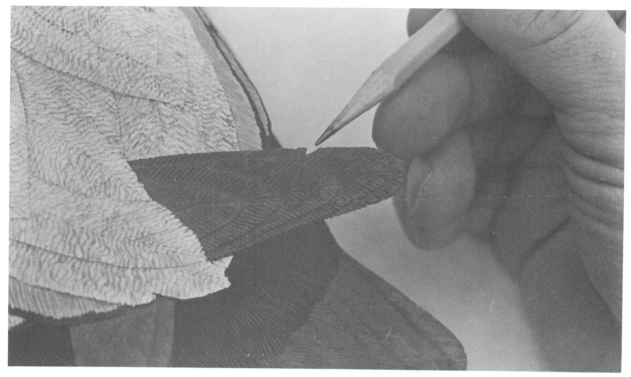

Illus. 189. Close-up of an inserted primary feather insert. Note the feather break.

Illus. 190. View of the primaries and tail.

Illus. 191. View of head and open bill.

11. Looking at a Red-Breasted Merganser

Illus. 192. The red-breasted merganser drake.

Illus. 193. Breast and shoulder area.

Illus. 194. View of side-pocket, secondaries, and primary wing feathers.

Illus. 195. Close-up of shoulder, side-pocket, and exposed wing coverts.

Illus. 196. Top view of back area showing the cape, scapular and tertial feathers.

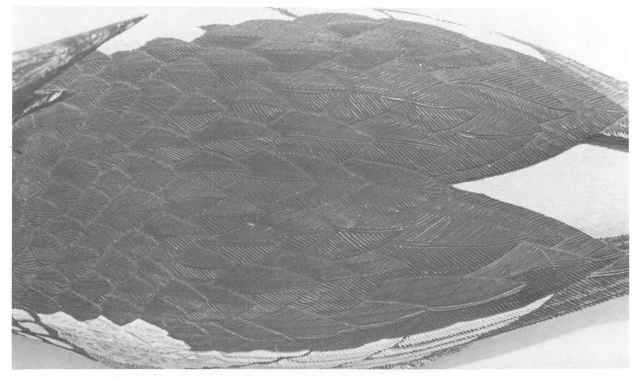

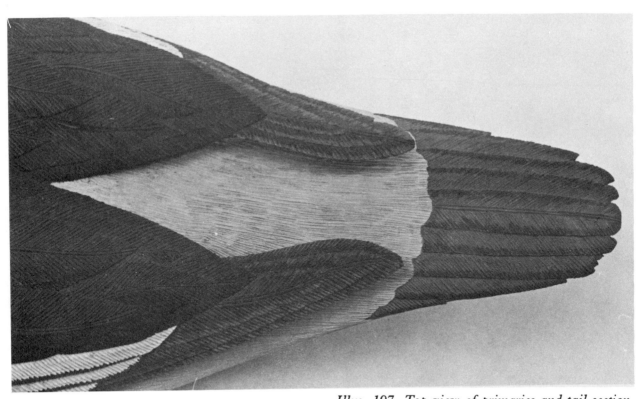

Illus. 197. Top view of primaries and tail section.

Illus. 198. Close-up of primary and the secondary feathers of the right wing.

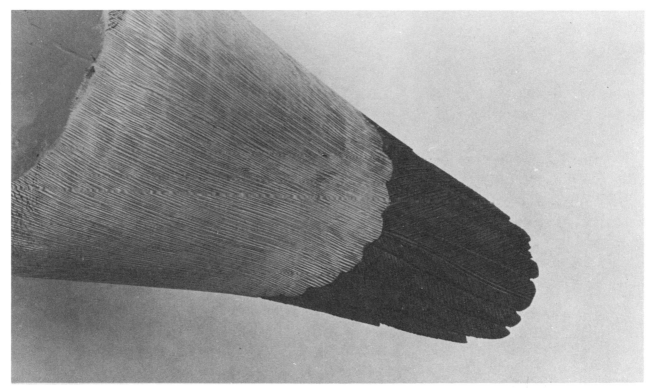

Illus. 199. Close-up of the underside of the tail.

Illus. 200. Head and bill.

12. Looking at the Mallard Drake

Illus. 201. The mallard drake (from the collection of William and "Bridie" Hickman).

Illus. 202. Neck, breast, and shoulder.

Illus. 203. Cape and scapular feathers. Note the fine vermiculations on the scapular area.

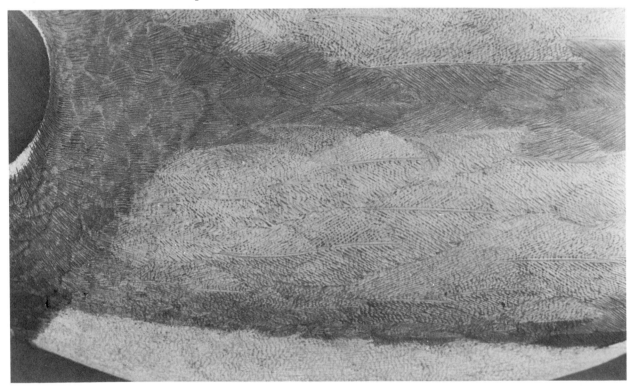

Illus. 204. Tertials, secondaries, and primary inserts.

Illus. 205. Scapulars, tertials, secondaries, and after section of the side pocket.

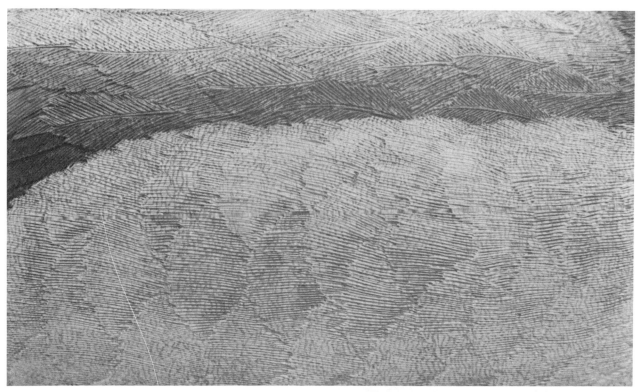

Illus. 206. Closeup view of where the scapulars and side pocket meet.

Illus. 207. Top view of the tertials, inserted primaries and tail section.

Illus. 208. Closeup view of the inserted oil-gland coverts.

Illus. 209. Lower tail coverts and underside view of the tail section.

Illus. 210. This pair of green-wing teal typify some of the techniques that can be incorporated into decoys made with clear transparent finishes. Photo by Jim Legault.

13. Advanced Techniques on Natural-Finished Decoys

Up to now, we have primarily dealt with realistic carving techniques on decoys that are to be painted. Many of these same techniques can be applied to carvings with natural finishes (Illus. 210). Some of the reasons for choosing a piece of wood that is to be used for a painted duck might be almost directly opposite the reasons for choosing woods that will be carved for natural-finished decoys.

Illus. 211. Defects such as knots, pitch pockets, color variances between heartwood and sapwood, wormholes, and similar degrades can often be worked to advantage and enhance the true natural look of a decoy carving.

Selecting wood for a natural carving allows the carver a much broader choice. Pieces of wood with some degree of knots and flaws no longer need be eliminated. These defects might, in fact, be used to enhance the carving (Illus. 211 and 212). Many more species of wood with various densities and grain configurations can be used, such as walnut, cherry, butternut, chestnut, and so on. The list can include any or all of the fine furniture woods. All of these woods generally have good carving and visual qualities which certainly interest the carver working with natural wood.

Illus. 212. Note the piece selected here for the head. It is actually from the center (pith) of the tree. Notice the circular pattern on the top of the bill created by the growth rings close to the pith.

Illus. 213. Joints and glue lines should be inconspicuous. The head and body pieces have similar grain patterns and color tones that help to make the glue joint less noticeable.

When working with natural wood, some new aspects enter into the picture. Tight joints and similar grain patterns in separate pieces is a must (Illus. 213). Avoid using or allowing any signs of wood putties or fillers to be visible on the finished decoy. Pieces of wood selected for the head, body, or inserts (if used) should all look alike in the finished carving. If one part is wormy, it's a good idea to have all parts wormy if possible. (See the hooded merganser shown in Illus. 214.) All man-made scratches must be totally removed from the surface of the carving. Sanding and more sanding becomes an absolute must as even minor man-made scratches or tool marks will detract greatly from the quality of the finished product.

However, positioning natural defects or flaws in certain locations can create an interesting aspect of the natural carving. Locating a knot on a crest or a swirling grain configuration on a wing area is something that must be planned when the carver lays the pattern on the wood. Planning with consideration for the best visual look of the end product must be worked on in the early stages of the work.

Illus. 214. Here pieces selected for the head, body, and even the inserts are all approximately equal in wormy density.

Illus. 215. An open bill adds considerable interest to a carving as shown on this blue-winged teal.

Illus. 216. This bluebill head shows a conventional pose with closed bill with some detailing.

Another freedom enjoyed by a natural wood carver is the choice to exaggerate or otherwise change any feature on the duck he desires. All natural decoys are, in reality, pieces of artistic sculpture. Consequently, the stringent guidelines that go into a realistic, painted decoy do not have to apply. Exacting, intricate details are no longer absolutely necessary. Over-detailing, in fact, may distract from the natural beauty of the wood itself and obscure nature's grain, color, and patterns—obliterating the very reasons one elects to do a natural decoy in the first place.

The Head

The area of the head always attracts the most visual attention. An open bill and very alert eyes as shown in Illus. 215 can create considerable interest. A relatively simple, shaped bill, carved from a beautifully patterned piece of wood can give a look of contour and smoothness as typified on the bluebill shown in Illus. 216. A carved eye (Illus. 217), can also be used effectively. Glass eyes may tend to draw one's visual attention away from the warmth and beauty of the wood.

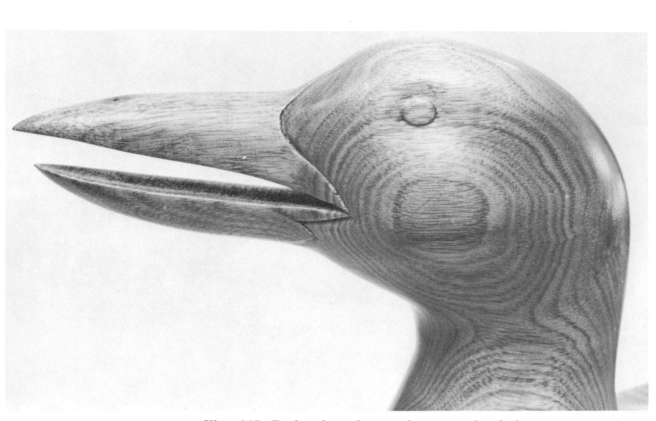

Illus. 217. Rather than always using conventional glass eyes try carving one as shown on this loon example.

Illus. 218 shows no extra details carved on the head whatsoever. Because of the interesting wood used in this work it was felt best to do little extra detailing so as not to make the patterns in the wood conflict or compete with carved details. Also, wormy wood can often be quite unstable or difficult to carve, so that intricate details such as carved eyes may be difficult to work in successfully. Know your piece of wood before you try special or unusual techniques. As previously mentioned, a lot of sanding is a must and this is especially true in the head area. A lot of end grain (Illus. 219), is exposed here which must be sanded very thoroughly. The head and/or bill is an excellent area where one might choose to exaggerate a specific feature of a duck. The shoveler shown in Illus. 220 normally has a large bill. In order to highlight this feature, the size of the bill was exaggerated. A carver can be creative and at the same time have some fun by departing from the strict proportions that normally govern the carving of realistic decoys.

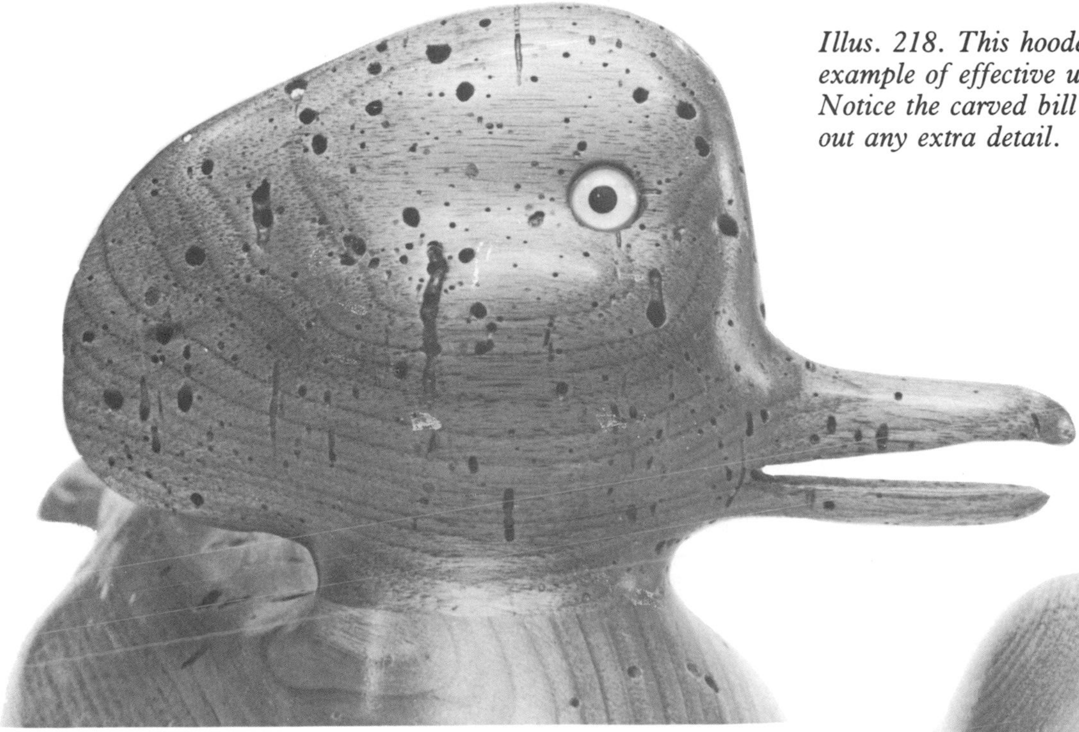

Illus. 218. This hooded merganser is an example of effective use of wormy wood. Notice the carved bill is without any extra detail.

Illus. 219. Here is a shot of a goldeneye, showing the nail and nostril details carved into solid wood. Note the "end grain" exposed on the head; an extensive sanding effort is required to get these surfaces perfectly smooth.

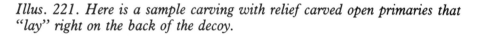

Illus. 220. The normally large bill of this shoveler has been exaggerated to call attention to that feature.

Illus. 221. Here is a sample carving with relief carved open primaries that "lay" right on the back of the decoy.

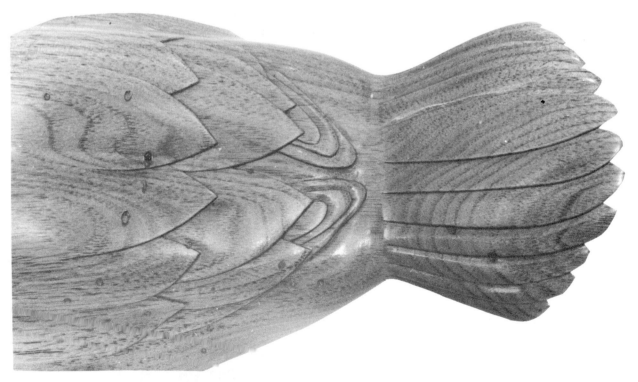

Scapulars, Tertials, and Wings

The feathers located in this area can be handled in many different ways. Several slightly relieved feathers are all that is necessary to give the illusion of wings. One can take this concept many steps further and create fairly complicated wings and still not lose the best features of the natural wood. The key to successful feather carving on natural wood is to use a very sharp knife. A sharp, smooth knife cut will eliminate a lot of sanding and make your job a lot easier. Illus. 221 shows the scapular, tertial, and primary feathers all relief-carved and lying entirely on the duck's body. Doing feathers in this manner requires no power tools at all. This technique certainly highlights the wing area. In Illus. 222, the area of the primary feathers are undercut and left open in order to give additional dimension to the carving. Note how smoothly the lines and surfaces of the feathers are.

Illus. 222. Undercutting raises or elevates the primaries off the back as shown here.

Illus. 223. Here is a view showing the effective, realistic results obtained on a natural decoy when inserted primaries are used.

Crossed primary inserts can also be used on a natural wood carving (Illus. 223). Elevated, crossed primaries are extremely difficult to carve from one piece and inserts, as we know, make the job easier. The wood used for the insert should match the body in color and grain. Make the inserts from the scrap pieces left over from the body cutout.

Inserts must fit into the grooves perfectly. After they have been glued in place, the groove shouldn't show at all. Any use of putty or filler here would detract from the natural beauty of the wood reducing the quality of the carving.

Illus. 224. A relief-carved wing (achieved by undercutting) shown in an exposed position.

An optional technique that can enhance your carving greatly is to totally expose a wing. (See Illus. 224.) It is an excellent way to add more interest and additional detail to the carving. Be sure to allow a little extra material to the pattern in this area so that there is enough stock for carving this type of wing.

Decoy carvings with extended wings (Illus. 225), can be some of the most graceful creations you can make. You will first need to draw and add a wing to your pattern. Make sure it is in the proper location and of the right proportions. Extended wings can be carved in any number of various new positions. The wing can be extended all the way, halfway, or not much at all. The position of the wing changes with the amount of its extension.

Illus. 225. This extended wing of a green-winged teal is not a separate insert, but carved from the same piece as the body. Photo by Jim Legault.

Tail Feathers

Carving each individual tail feather is another relatively easy-to-do technique that gives a personalized and creative dimension to your carving. The bluebill tail shown in Illus. 226 has also been carved in a slightly fanned position and each feather has been carved to highlight this effect.

The large fanned tail of the ruddy duck is another example (Illus. 227). If the tail is carved in a vertical or diagonal position, the carver can utilize the cross-grained pattern of the wood (Illus. 228), to add even more beauty to the surface pattern of the carving.

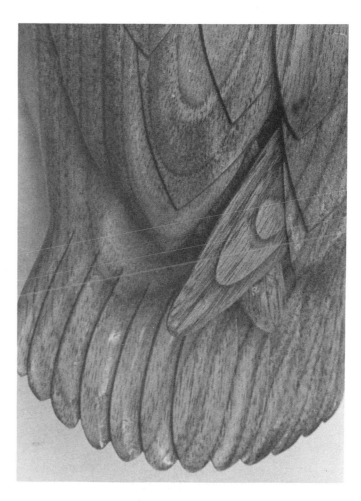

Illus. 226. Each individual tail feather can be carved as on this bluebill.

Illus. 227. Top view of a fanned tail carved on a ruddy duck.

179

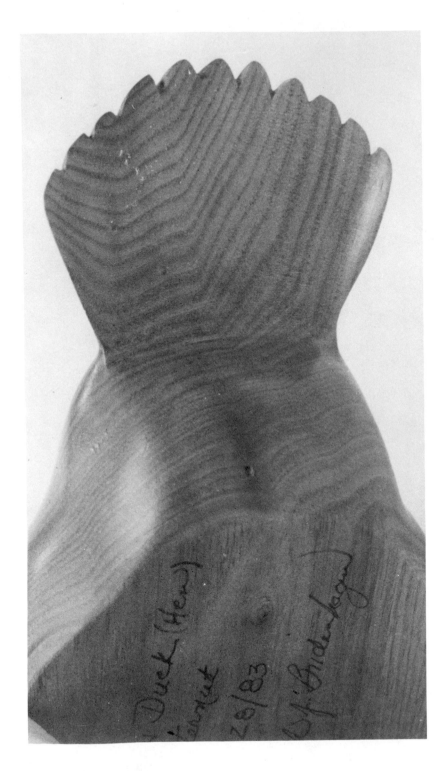

Illus. 228. Bottom view of the tail in Illus. 227. This shows the cross-graining pattern. It must be carved carefully to avoid breakage.

Illus. 229. Carved feet of matching wood is an effect many carvers don't deal with.

Carved Feet

A standing carving adds a whole new dimension in shape contour, and depth. Feet made from matching pieces of wood can be carved and attached to the body (Illus. 229). These additional wood pieces that extend away from the body are best reinforced with hardwood dowels as shown in Illus. 230. These dowels run through the feet and into the duck's body. Allow enough dowel length to extend through the bottom of the feet to help in securing or mounting the carving to a base.

The possibilities for carving different poses and attitudes in natural-finished carvings is almost endless.

Illus. 230. Reinforce "add-ons" with concealed dowels when extra strength is required. The extra dowel length is for extending into a base.

There is a great variety of different kinds of wood finishes that can be applied to natural carvings. These include various oils, varnishes, lacquers, and polyurethanes. The choice is yours. Illus. 231 through 249 is a photo gallery illustrating a number of different decoys with some extra closeup views. These photo examples show results and some of the special features characteristic to beautiful natural-finished decoys.

Illus. 231. A full-view hooded merganser in wormy butternut.

Illus. 232. Full view of a bluebill.

Illustrations on opposite page.

Illus. 233 (top). Rear details on the bluebill.

Illus. 234 (bottom). Top view of the bluebill's back shows the "swirling" grain pattern that is automatically obtained from contouring the wood through its growth layers.

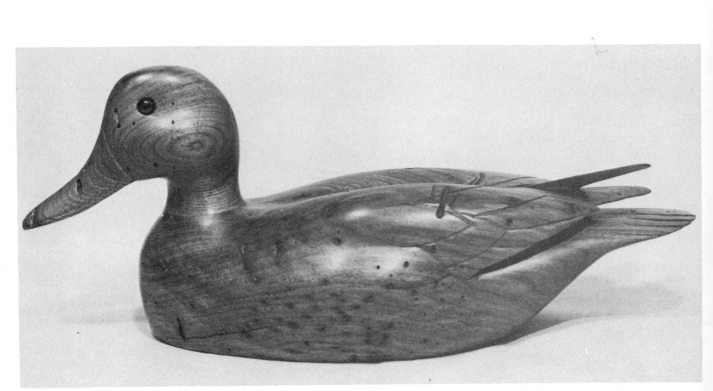

Illus. 235. This view of a mallard hen shows a fairly wormy surface.

Illus. 236. The opposite view of the same mallard hen is much less wormy as dictated by the character of the wood.

Illus. 237. Goldeneye.
Illus. 238. Close-up of the goldeneye head.

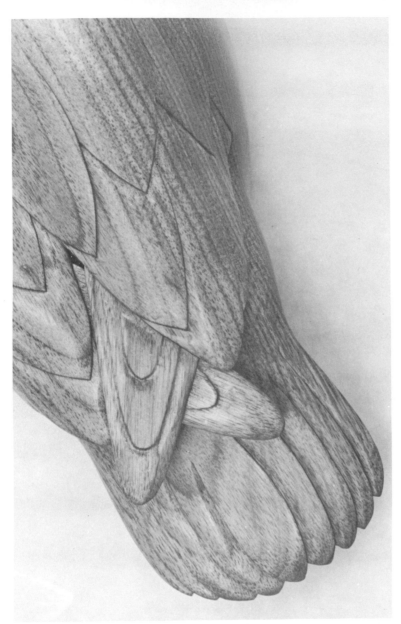

Illus. 239. Inserted crossed primaries and carved tail area of the goldeneye.

Illus. 240. The blue-winged teal with an exposed wing.

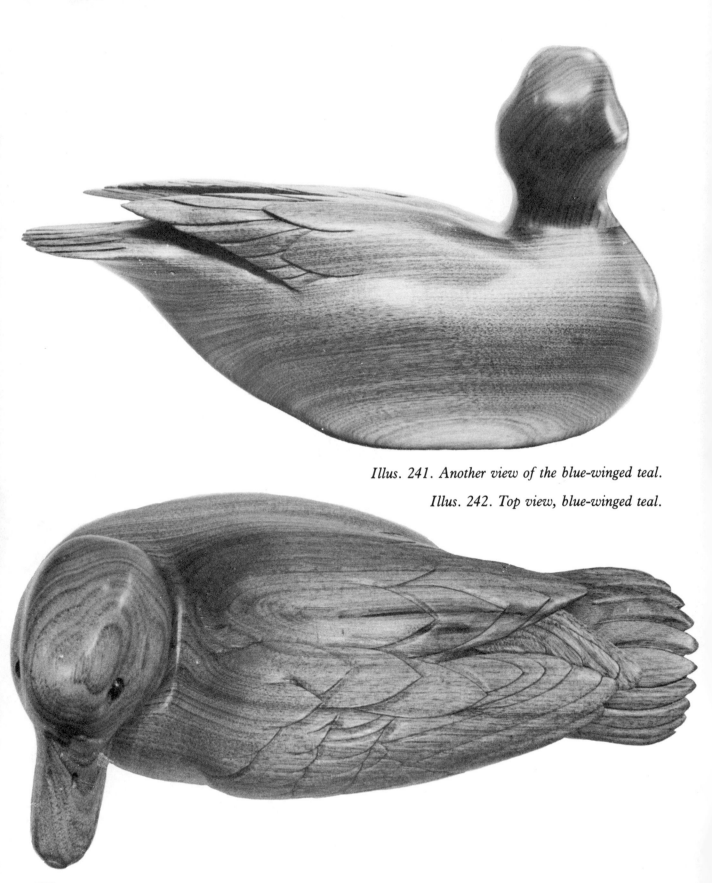

Illus. 241. Another view of the blue-winged teal.

Illus. 242. Top view, blue-winged teal.

Illus. 243. Ruddy duck.

Illus. 244. Head of the ruddy duck.

Illus. 245. Common loon.

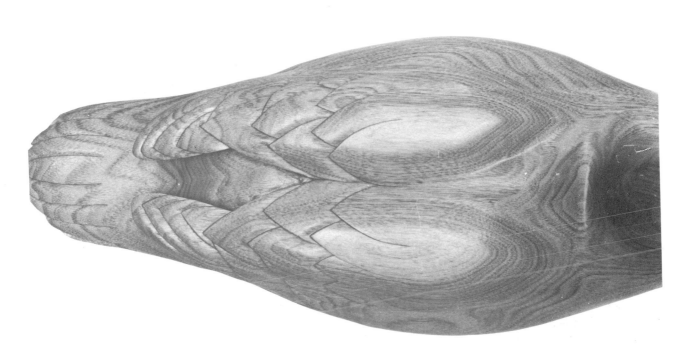

Illus. 246. Body top view of the common loon.

Illus. 247. Detailed view of the carved scapulars on the common loon.

Illus. 248. Standing shoveler.

Illus. 249. Another view of the shoveler.

Conclusion

In the final analysis, we hope the photo studies and information contained here will be of valuable assistance to the carver in pursuit of improving his ability as an artist. If we can leave you with three thoughts on the subject, we wouldn't want you to forget, they would include:

Be Patient—Don't rush your work. Some of the procedures simply take time and can only be done slowly—hair by hair and stroke by stroke.

Be an Innovator—Always take the time to try out new ideas and test new methods. Just because you've not seen an idea in a book doesn't mean your approach cannot be an accepted or valid procedure. All ideas and techniques come from somewhere. There is no reason why one of your ideas can't be a first and if you share it with others it may become an established technique for the benefit of all decoy artists.

Study—As you progress in this art form, let the study of waterfowl become an obsession. The only way to truly understand the anatomy and attitudes of various species is to watch them behave in person. You will begin to understand the ways of the "marsh." Your carvings will become proportionally better in authenticity and better in overall visual quality. But, beyond this something greater will happen. You will understand the importance of wetlands and help make our world better for future generations.

APPENDICES

I. Decoy Contests and Shows

As you progress as a carver, you may want to consider entering one of the many decoy contests which take place all across the United States and Canada. (At this time, these contests seem to be popular only in North America.) You can enter these contests in one of two ways. You can take your entry to the contest or you can ship it to the contest with your entry blank, entry fee, and return-shipping costs. There are advantages and disadvantages to both methods.

The most obvious advantage in going to the contest personally is being able to witness firsthand the scrutiny a duck must pass to win a ribbon. The ducks are usually judged by the best panel of carvers around. Each decoy is checked over detail by detail. Attending the contest enables you to talk to other carvers, to discuss techniques, and to share ideas for your next creations. Being able to see other people's work is an opportunity to judge for yourself how well your carving rates in the competition. This can be an invaluable inspiration.

If contests are not located in your immediate area, it can become quite costly to start attending them. It will usually require travel, meals, and motel or hotel rooms. Mailing an entry can eliminate these costs, but it also has its drawbacks. First of all one loses the contact one would have with the show and other carvers. Another problem is that one always stands the chance of having one's work damaged in shipment to or from the contest. The third problem is probably the greatest of all—the wait!

First of all you ship the carving at least two weeks before the show so you are sure it gets there in time. Then the date of the contest arrives and you don't hear a word. Then you wait another two to three weeks and finally you get your carving back. You carefully open the box and immediately notice that the tip of a tail feather has broken off. As you sift through the plastic foam chips for the third time you realize that there is no ribbon and no slip of paper telling you the reason why. All you see is a number stuck to the bottom of your decoy.

This sort of happening is not entirely the fault of the contest. Contests have become so popular and have grown so rapidly that most are very understaffed and underbudgeted no matter how hard their dedicated volunteers work. It is impossible for them to write an analysis of each duck and state why it won or didn't win. If you are looking for a challenge, entering a contest is certainly the way to find one.

Contest Rules
Contests have definite sets of rules and special categories that one must abide by. These rules are usually clearly laid out in the entry blank you must send for before the show. More and more contests are insisting that all parts of a carving must be made of wood unless they are essential to the support structure of a decorative piece. In this case they may allow you to use a metal rod of some sort. The matter is totally left up to the judges' discretion.

Cast Pewter Feet and real duck's feet as shown in Illus. 250 are not allowed, nor can a carver use cast bills. The one part of the anatomy not made of wood that is acceptable are glass eyes.

If one enters the competition class which is usually broken down into Professional, Amateur, and Novice grades, the duck must be balanced perfectly. It is judged while floating in large tanks of water.

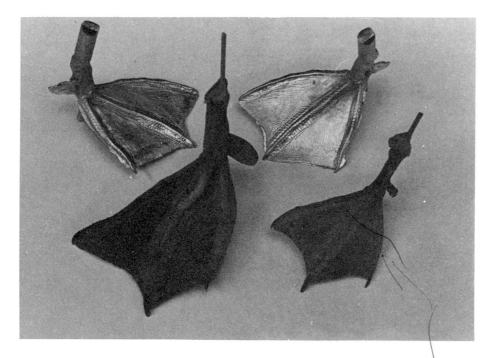

Illus. 250. A set of cast pewter feet compared to the two preserved ones from a real duck, in the foreground.

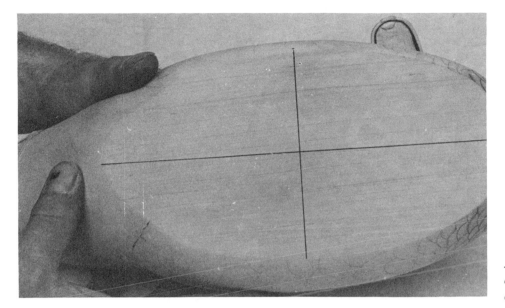

Illus. 251. After carving, divide the body into quadrants.

Any tipping or listing or checking that appears is an immediate disqualification. Weighting a duck so that it floats properly is done as follows:

After all the basic carving has been completed and the duck has been sanded to proper shape, turn the duck over and divide the bottom into quadrants as shown in Illus. 251. Now float the duck in a

Illus. 252. Secure a thin lead weight with a rubber band, then test float it again.

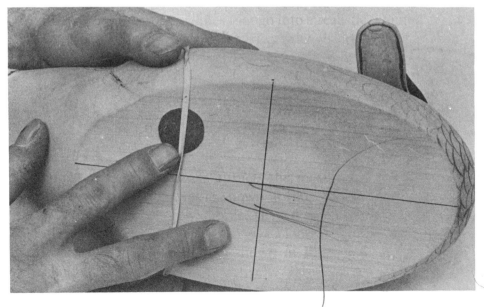

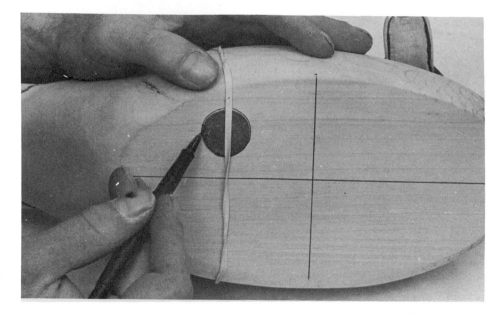

Illus. 253. Outline the weight after it has been properly positioned.

large sink or bathtub and determine which quadrant is riding at the highest level. Secure a thin lead disc (Illus. 252) temporarily with a rubber band and test float again. You may find that more than one disc is necessary. Once you have the duck floating evenly on the water, outline the location of the weight (Illus. 253). Illus. 254 shows the recessing of the outlined area to the necessary depth. The lead weight is secured in place with glue (Illus. 255) and filled in with putty.

Illus. 254. Carve a recess to the appropriate depth.

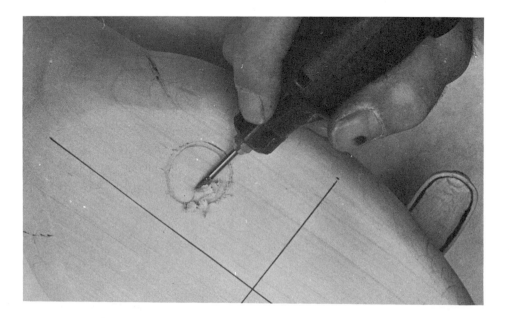

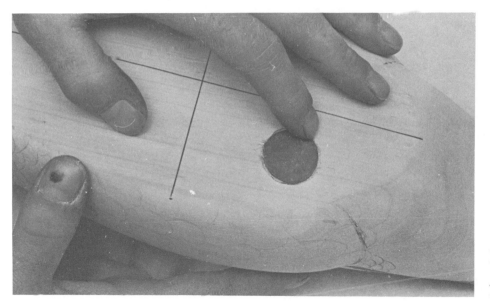

Illus. 255. Secure the weight with a waterproof glue and fill in any voids with putty.

It is absolutely necessary to properly seal the surface of a duck that is to be floated to avoid any checking or cracking. Even though most contests adopt basically the same rules, some minor variations do occur and the carver should be aware of any unusual differences. The locations and months of some of the popular and well-established decoy shows and contests are listed here for your convenience and interest.

The Ward Foundation World Championship
Convention Hall,
Ocean City, Maryland

Held in April

U.S. National Decoy Show
Melville, Long Island

Held in March

Pacific Flyway Decoy Association Wildfowl
    Festival
Red Lion Motor Inn
2001 Point West Way
Sacramento, California

Held in June

International Wildlife Carving Exposition
World Congress Center
Atlanta, Georgia

Held in April

Catahoula Lake Festival
Kees Park Community Center
Pineville, Louisiana

Held in October

Northside Lions Wildfowl Carving and Art
    Exhibition
State Fairgrounds
Richmond, Virginia

Held in February

Easton Waterfowl Festival
Easton, Maryland

Held in November

Pacific Southwest Wildfowl Arts Festival
(formerly the California Open)
Embarcadero Convention Center
San Diego, California

Held in February

The North American Wildfowl Carving
   Championship
Pointe Mouillee State Game Area
Route Z
Rockwood, Michigan

Held in September

Ohio Decoy Collectors and Carvers Show
% Ohio Decoy Collectors and Carvers Assoc.
P.O. Box 29224
Parma, Ohio

Held in March

The Wisconsin Decoy Collectors Show
The Pioneer Inn
Oshkosh, Wisconsin

Held in March

II. Special Tooling

There are a few special items that are very helpful and practically considered essentials by the serious carver. These include (in addition to common woodworking tools) miniature power tools, basic rotary cutters, small files, and burning tools.

High-speed *miniature power tools* like the popular Dremel tool or a flexible shaft, handpiece, and power unit such as one of the Foredom models shown in Illus. 256 certainly speeds and simplifies all detailed carving jobs. Better handpieces have interchangeable collets that allow the operator to use a variety of cutters with shank diameters from

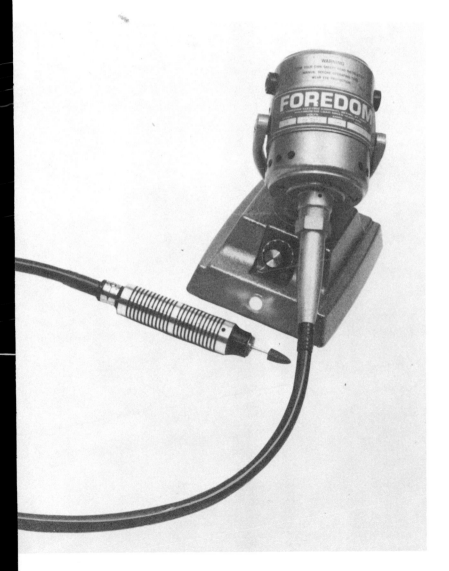

Illus. 256. The Foredom variable-speed, miniature, power-tool, flexible-shaft machine with handpiece that handles collets from 1/16 to 1/4 inch in size.

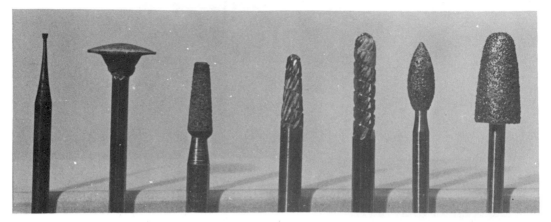

Illus. 257. A basic selection of cutters for miniature power-tool work. The two at far right are ruby stones.

one-sixteenth to one-fourth of an inch. Hundreds of rotary cutters in different configurations (Illus. 257) are available for the miniature power tools, including various burrs, grinders, sanding points, and so on—all available from the usual woodcraft tooling supply sources.

Illus. 258. Structured carbide burrs. Taper shape at left with two sphere shapes.

Among the newest types of rotary cutters that have been getting much attention and are generally endorsed by professional carvers are the *structured carbide burrs* (Illus. 258). Sold under the trade name of "Karbide Kutzall," and manufactured by the L.R. Oliver Co., each of these cutters has numerous needlelike teeth structured of tungsten carbide. They cut all woods cleanly, penetrate easily, and remove stock quickly without burning. The Kutzall bits come in various sizes ranging from one-eighth- to three-quarter-inch cutting diameters. They are currently available in these basic shapes: taper, ball nose, sphere, cylinder, and rotary saw. Shanks are either one-eighth- or one-fourth-inch diameters.

Ruby stone rotary tools (Illus. 257) were actually designed for the dental industry, but have been found to be great for fine detailing and

Illus. 259. Needle rasps.

shaping work in wood. These cutters also come in many shapes and configurations. They are usually available from suppliers that handle cutters and burrs for miniature power tools.

Needle rasps (Illus. 259) in various cross-sectional shapes are similar to the machinist's needle files, but cut much faster because they are designed specifically for woodworking. Needle rasps are especially useful to reach areas such as undercuts that cannot otherwise be worked with knives or power tools. Small flat rasps are also better to use than rotary-power cutting tools for final shaping of convex surfaces such as bills.

Feather burning tools will precisely place uniformly fine, delicately spaced, incised lines in texturing, and the realistic detailing is more accurately, faster, and most easily accomplished with a quality feather burner. This is the most important single item necessary for producing realistic carvings. Electric wood-burning tools available today encompass a wide range of capabilities and investment costs. Most professionals do insist upon having an accessory control that allows dialing down the tip temperature for fine incisions or can be cranked

Illus. 260. The Hot Tool.

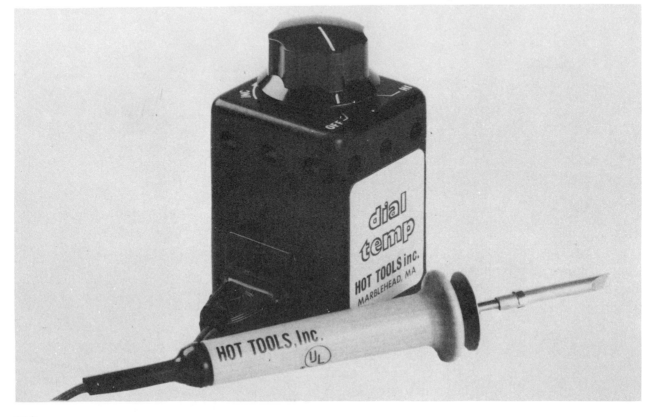

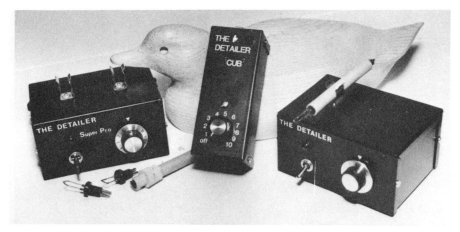

Illus. 261. Control-unit models available from Colwood Electronics, left to right: "Super Pro," "Cub," and the standard "Detailer."

up for hot, fast, deep incisions. Different kinds of surfaces and various species of wood and different desires in artistic expression require a broad range of heat adjustments and various shapes of tips.

Popular brand names associated with feather-burning tools include "Hot Tools" (Illus. 260), and the "Detailer" (Illus. 261–265).

Illus. 262. Closeup look at the Detailer, handpiece, and basic tip shapes for feather burning.

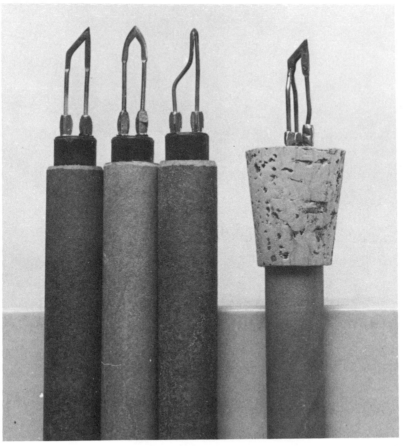

Illus. 263. A closeup look at the basic burning tips. The one at the right has a double edge which speeds the feather-texturing process.

Illus. 264. Two types of handpieces for the detailers. Above is the fixed tip, below is the interchangeable tip model.

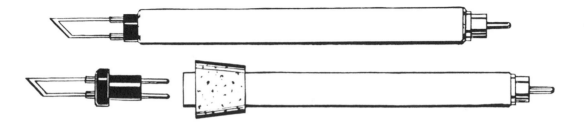

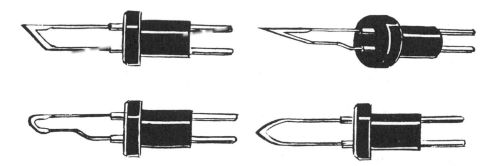

Illus. 265. Four of fourteen tip shapes available. Above: Pointed and spear for general feather burning. Below: Round and spade tips. Rounded tips are ideal for concaved surfaces such as under the neck and so on.

The "Hot Tool" burner is a general-purpose economical unit in a penlike handpiece that may be purchased with or without an optional rheostat temperature control. It has several differently shaped interchangeable tips that must be purchased separately. Tips are easily changed with a simple slip-on system that keeps the tip in place without threads or screws.

The "Detailer" is one of a family of three variable-heat woodburning systems manufactured by Colwood Electronics (Illus. 261). All of their models consist of separate, slim-line handpieces (Illus. 262–265) and cord connected to a control unit. Colwood offers their economy "Cub" unit, the standard model "Detailer," and their deluxe detailer called the "Super-Pro." All are designed especially for precise feather-texturing jobs. Their best model comes with a heavyduty handpiece with the capability of burning deep incisions for installing feather inserts.

III. Sources for Special Supplies and Tooling

Sources for special supplies and tooling, including wood blocks, pre-carved kits, eyes, study bills, and cast feet along with the new carbide carving burrs and feather burners are listed here for your convenience. Time and space forced us to limit these sources to ones in North America.

Some of these not-so-common items are available by mail from a few of the familiar and long-standing companies. However some of the items are only currently available from the small, "one-man" (so to speak), mail-order companies. These small companies occasionally change names, change locations, or just come and go with changes in economical climate or for other reasons. Consequently, the long-term validity of this information may be subject to question. Thus, we request not to be held responsible should there ever happen to be some difficulty in correspondence or in other matters.

When dealing with any mail-order supplier it is obviously best to write for current prices and catalogues while at the same time verifying the existence of the company. The list here does not include sources for common tools and supplies such as rotary and other power or hand tools (flexible shafts, files, etc.), paints, finishes, or brushes. Such items are readily available locally at good arts and crafts and hobby shops, or from conventional mail-order sources—including some of those listed in this book.

Distributors of Supplies and Tooling

Unfinished Decoys and Kits

Artistry in Veneers, Inc.
Audubon Workshop
Bay Country Woodcrafts, Inc.
Bird Carving America
Constantine & Son, Inc.
Kent Courtney's Wood Shed
Forest Products
Great Northern Decoy Co.
Jerry's
Rolfe's Woodworks
Spielmans Woodworks
Woodcraft Supply Corp.
Woodworker Supply of New Mexico

Special Carving Blocks and Lumber

Chez La Rogue (Tupelo)
Constantine & Son, Inc.
Kent Courtney's Wood Shed (Tupelo)
Craft Woods (Jelutong, Basswood)
P. C. English Enterprises (Tupelo, Buckeye)
J. H. Kline Carving Shop (Basswood, Butternut)
Northwest Carving Supplies
Uncle Al's Wood Products (K. D. Basswood, Cedar)
Dick Watson (Jelutong, Cedar)
Wildlife Carving Supply

Glass Eyes

Chez La Rogue
Christian J. Hummel Co.
Craft Woods
P. C. English Enterprises
Forest Products
B. Frame Co.

Hutch Decoy Carving, Ltd.
Jerry's
J. H. Kline Carving Shop
Lewis Tool & Supply Co.
Rolfe's Woodworks
Schoepfer Eyes
Tohickon Glass Eyes
Traders Den Taxidermy
VanDyke Supply Co.
Dick Watson
West Coast Taxidermist Supply Co.
Wildlife Carving Supply

Study Bills

Craft Woods
Oscar Johnston Wildlife Gallery
J. H. Kline Carving Shop
Bob Miller
Dick Watson
Wildlife Carving Supply

Carbide Carving Burrs ("Kutzall")

P. C. English Enterprises
J. H. Kline Carving Shop
Lewis Tool and Supply Co.
L. R. Oliver & Co., Inc.
Sculpture Associates Ltd., Inc.
Joe Veracka & Associates
Wildlife Carving Supply
Dick Watson
Wood Carvers Supply Co.
Woodcraft Supply Corp.
The Wood Works

Feather Burning Tools

Artistry in Veneers, Inc.
Chesterfield Craft Shop
Chez La Rogue
Colwood Electronics
Kent Courtney's Wood Shed
Craft Woods
Garrett-Wade
Hot Tools, Inc.
J. H. Kline Carving Shop
Leichtung, Inc.
Lewis Tool and Supply Co.
Northwest Carving Supplies
Joe Veracka & Associates

Wildlife Carving Supplies
Wood Carvers Supply Co.
Woodcraft Supply Corp.
Wood-Knots Distributors

Cast Feet

Craft Woods
Richard Delise
Forest Products
J. H. Kline Carving Shop
Lewis Tool and Supply Co.
Northwest Carving Supplies
Rolfe's Woodworks
Wildlife Carving Supply

IV. Companies and Suppliers— Addresses

Christian J. Hummel Co.
P.O. Box 2877
Baltimore, MD 21225

Artistry in Veneers
633 Montauk Ave.
Brooklyn, NY 11208

Colwood Electronics
715 West Wood Ave.
Long Branch, NJ 07740

Audubon Workshop
1501 Paddock Dr.
Northbrook, IL 60062

Constantine & Son, Inc.
2050 Eastchester Rd.
Bronx, NY 10461

Bay Country Woodcrafts, Inc.
U.S. Route 13
Oak Hall, VA 23416

Kent Courtney's Woodshed
625 W. Main
Broussard, LA 70518

Bird Carving America
Box 468
Cataumet, Cape Cod, Mass. 02534

Craft Woods
York Rd. & Beaver Run La.
Cockeysville, MD 21030

Birds of a Feather
Box 456-A
Caroga Lake, NY 12032

Richard Delise
920 Springwood Dr.
Westchester, PA 19380

Chesterfield Craft Shop
Box 208 Chesterfield
Trenton, NJ 08620

P. C. English Enterprises
Rt. 1, Box 136
Fredericksburg, VA 22401

Chez La Rogue
Hwy. 59 So.
Rt. 3, Box 148
Foley, AL 36535

Forest Products
P.O. Box 12
Avon, OH 44011

B. Frame Co.
169 Schan Dr.
Churchville, PA 18966

Great Northern Decoy Co.
P.O. Box 53
Linthicum, MD 21090

Hot Tools Inc.
7 Hawkes St.
P.O. Box 53
Marblehead, Mass. 01945

Hutch Decoy Carving, Ltd.
7715 Warsaw Ave.
Clen Burnie, MD 21061

Jerry's
19536 W. 7 Mi. Rd.
Northville, MI 48167

Oscar Johnston Wildlife Gallery
Rt. 2 Box 1224
Smith River, CA 95567

J. H. Kline Carving Shop
R.D. 2 Forge Hill Road
Manchester, PA 17345

Lee Valley Tools
2680 Queensview Dr.
Ottawa, Ontario
Canada K2B 8J9

Leichtung, Inc.
4944 Commerce Parkway
Cleveland, OH 44128

Lewis Tool & Supply (Catalog $1)
912 W. 8th St.
Loveland, CO 80537

Master Paint Systems
P.O. Box 1320
Loganville, GA 30249

Bob Miller
General Delivery
Evergreen, LA 71333

Norta, Inc.
113 Ave. F
Lodi, NJ 07644

Northwest Carving Supplies
P.O. Box 5211
Bozeman, MT 59715

L. R. Oliver & Co., Inc.
4645 Bree Rd.
St. Clair, MI 48079

Rolfe's Woodworks
6905 River Birch Dr.
Raleigh, NC 27612

Schoepfer Eyes
138 West 31st St.
New York, NY 10001

Sculpture Associates Ltd.
114 East 25th St.
New York, NY 10001

Spielmans Woodworks
188 Gibraltar Rd.
Fish Creek, WI 54212

Tohickon Glass Eyes
Box 15
Erwinna, PA 18920

Traders Den Taxidermy
131 Sacramento, JCT 64 & 23
Sycamore, IL 60178

Uncle Al's Wood Products
214 Chestnut St.
Oconto Falls, WI 54154

VanDyke Supply Co.
Woonsocket, SD 57385

Joe Veracka & Associates
P.O. Box 48962
Chicago, IL 60648-0962

Garrett Wade
161 Ave. of the Americas
New York, NY 10013

Walnut Hollow Farm
Route 2
Dodgeville, WI 53533

Dick Watson
8800 Anchor Bay
Fair Haven, MI 48023

West Coast Taxidermist Supply Co.
648 San Mateo Ave.
San Brano, CA 94066

Wildlife Carving Supply
317 Holyoke Ave.
Beach Haven, NJ 08008

Wood Carvers Supply Co.
3056 Excelsior Blvd.
Mineapolis, Minn. 55416

Woodcraft Supply Corp.
41 Atlantic Ave., Box 4000
Woburn, MA 01888

Wood-Knots Distributors
805 Garden of the Gods Rd.
Colorado Springs, CO 80907

The Woodworkers Store
21801 Industrial Blvd.
Rogers, MN 55374

Woodworkers Supply of New Mexico
5604 Alameda N.E.
Albuquerque, NM 87113

The Woodworks
2625 E. Louise Dr.
Phoenix, AZ 85032

V. Bibliography

BOOKS

Bellrose, Frank C. *Ducks, Geese, & Swans of North America*. Harrisburg, PA: Stackpole Books, 1976

Berry, Bob. *Decoy Patterns*. Robert G. Berry, 1983

Burk, Bruce. *Waterfowl Studies*. Piscataway, NJ: Winchester Press, 1976

——. *Game Bird Carving*. Piscataway, NJ: Winchester Press, Revised Edition, 1982

Frank, Charles W. *Anatomy of a Waterfowl for Carvers & Painters*. Gretna, LA: Pelican Publishing Co., 1982

Heintzelman, Donald S. *North American Ducks, Geese, & Swans*. Piscataway, NJ: Winchester Press, 1978

Lansdowne, J. F. *Birds of the West Coast, Vol. II*. Boston: Houghton Mifflin Company, 1980

LeMaster, Richard. *Waterfowl: the artist's guide to anatomy, attitude, & color*. Chicago: Contemporary Books, Inc., 1983

——. *Wildlife in Wood*. Chicago: Contemporary Books, Inc., 1978

——. *The LeMaster Method*. Scotch Game Call Co., Inc.

Moyer, John W. *Practical Taxidermy*. New York: John Wiley & Sons, Inc., 1979

Ponte, Alfred M. *26 Realistic Duck Patterns*. The Lincoln Press, 1982

Smithe, Frank B. *Naturalist's Color Guide*, New York: The American Museum of Natural History, 1975

Spielman, Patrick. *Making Wood Decoys*. New York: Sterling Publishing Co., Inc., 1982

Tawes, William I. *Creative Bird Carving*. Centreville, MD: Tidewater Publishers, 1969

Todd, Frank S. *Waterfowl: Ducks, Geese, & Swans of the World*. New York: Harcourt Brace Jovanovich Inc., 1979

Veasey, William. *Waterfowl Painting: Blue Ribbon Techniques*. Exton, PA: Schiffer Publishing Ltd., 1983

——, with Hull, Cary Schuler. *Waterfowl Carving: Blue Ribbon Techniques*. Exton, PA: Schiffer Publishing Ltd., 1982

PERIODICALS

Audubon magazine, National Audubon Society, 950 Third Ave., New York, NY, 10022

Breakthrough magazine, quarterly, devoted to the serious wildlife artist. Contains articles on decoy carving, reference materials, taxidermy, sculpting, base-making, buying guides, etc. Published at P.O. 1320, Loganville, GA 30249

The Decoy Hunter, 6 issues yearly. Primarily devoted to buying and selling, decoy auctions, and information for collectors. Published at 901 N. 9th St., Clinton, Ind. 47842

Decoy magazine, quarterly, deals with decoy collecting and carving. Articles feature carvers, artists, shows, competitions, and collections. Write P.O. Box 1900, Montego Bay Station, Ocean City, MD 21842

Ducks Unlimited, bimonthly magazine by Ducks Unlimited, 1 Waterfowl Way at Gilmer Rd., Long Grove, IL 60047

Ward Foundation News, quarterly by The Ward Foundation and the North American Wildfowl Art Museum, Salisbury State College, Salisbury, MD 21801. The Ward Foundation (Nonprofit) is dedicated to advancing wildfowl carving and painting. They sponsor carving competitions, art exhibits, and the world wildfowl carving championships.

Waterfowlers' World, bimonthly, excellent photos—most articles deal with hunting. Waterfowlers' World, 3540 Summer Ave., Suite 410, Memphis, TN 38122

Index